GETTING **STARTED**
crochet

Judith L. **Swartz**

INTERWEAVE PRESS

Project editor: Ayleen Stellhorn
Technical editor: Jean Lampe
Cover and interior design: Paulette Livers
Production: Pauline Brown
Photography: Joe Coca
Illustration: Ann Swanson
Photo styling: Ann Swanson
Proofreader and indexer: Nancy Arndt

Interweave Press LLC
201 East Fourth Street
Loveland, CO 80537-5655 USA
www.interweave.com

Printed and bound in China through Asia Pacific
Library of Congress Cataloging-in-Publication Data

Swartz, Judith L., 1953-
  Getting started crochet / Judith L. Swartz, author.
      p. cm.
  Includes index.
  ISBN 1-59668-006-7 (hardbound)
  ISBN-13: 978-1-59668-006-7
  1. Crocheting. 2. Crocheting--Patterns. I. Title.
  TT820.S96 2006
  746.43'4--dc22
                                    2006002646

10 9 8 7 6 5 4 3 2 1

acknowledgments

This book is dedicated to the memory of my wonderful parents, Claire and Alexander Swartz, for all they taught me, for always believing in me and encouraging me to follow my passions. Not a day goes by without missing them.

Writing a book is a multifaceted process requiring a team effort. This book would not have been possible without the fabulous team I have been fortunate enough to work with. My gratitude goes out to Ayleen Stellhorn, my editor. Thank you for your patience, kindness, and understanding along with your excellent editing and writing skills. I am also very grateful for the opportunity, once again, to work with Jean Lampe, my technical editor. You are the absolute authority on crochet knowledge, and what you don't know you have the ability to ferret out. Along with your eagle eyes, I must add detective to your list of qualifications. Thank you to Rebecca Campbell, managing editor at Interweave, for your support and understanding of the challenges of writing a book when life pulls you in multiple directions and for all your untiring efforts to keep me on track. Thanks to all of you for not giving up on me.

Special thanks go out to many people at Interweave Press, including Linda Stark for her enthusiasm in this project and her belief in my abilities. Thanks also to Betsy Armstrong and to the entire book production staff for their consistent excellence in creating quality books. It is a pleasure to work with all of you. Thank you to my dear friend Marilyn Murphy, a leader in her field, who continues to inspire me. I am very grateful to have the opportunity to combine work with friendship.

Thanks to Peggy Saewert for her excellent crochet skills. Thank you also to the yarn companies who supplied the materials for these projects. It is always a pleasure to work with fine materials.

Personal thanks are necessary as well. First and foremost to my wonderful husband, Joel Marcus, not only for his love, support, and understanding, but also for giving me the time and space necessary to complete this project. I am, indeed, a very lucky woman. Thanks to my sister, Susan Fish, for her moral support, and to all my wonderful friends whose advice and understanding I appreciate more than you will ever know. Last, I must acknowledge my dear dog and cat, Sandy and Miriam, whose contentedness to just stay near and watch me crochet is a great joy in my life.

contents

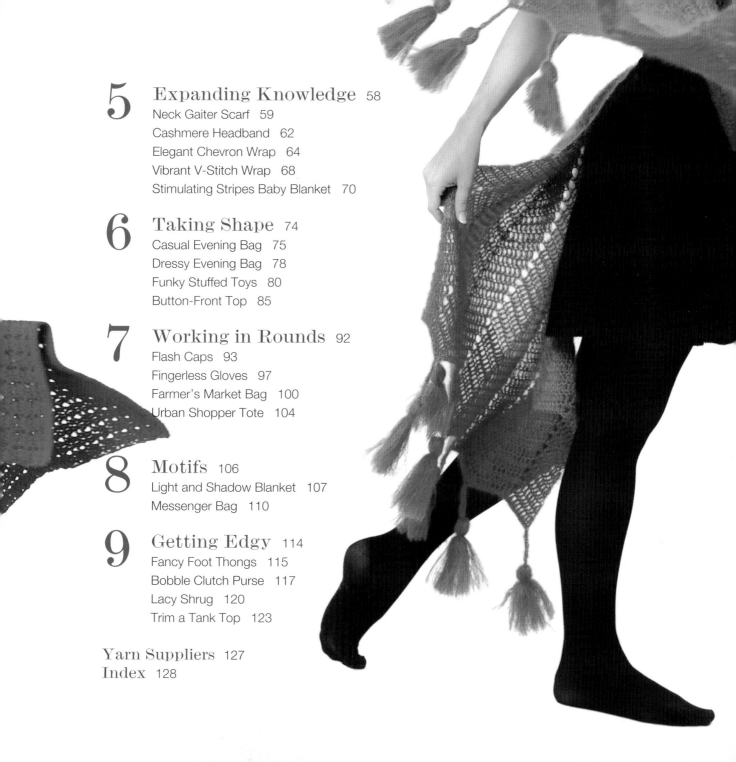

introduction

Perhaps it was the oh-so-chic woman you passed on the street with the fabulous lacy scarf trailing after her. Maybe it was a colorful blanket you remember curling up in as a child, feeling safe from the world. Or maybe you are feeling the need to de-stress and the idea of doing something constructive with your hands sounds very satisfying.

Maybe you've attempted to crochet in the past only to encounter obstacles, such as overstimulation in the yarn store (leading to confusion instead of inspiration) or a salesperson who spoke in such jargon that you ended up with that "I don't even know what I don't know" feeling.

For whatever reason, you have the desire to crochet and now you need to know how to go about it. How do you get from inspiration to finished product?

By picking up *Getting Started Crochet,* you have come to the right place. This is the book to start with. We'll go step by step, taking you through all the necessary information. You will learn the language of crochet and then how to abbreviate it. You will learn the basic stitches (there are really

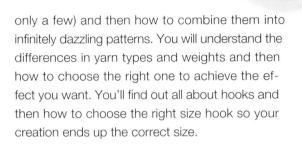

only a few) and then how to combine them into infinitely dazzling patterns. You will understand the differences in yarn types and weights and then how to choose the right one to achieve the effect you want. You'll find out all about hooks and then how to choose the right size hook so your creation ends up the correct size.

Crochet is a technique that is relatively easy to learn. Because it is so basic, it offers a great foundation for creativity. The simplicity of many of the projects in this book makes them a perfect canvas for personalization. Use your imagination when adding the finishing touches to individualize the look. Once you master a few projects, you will be on your way to designing your own.

This book offers a variety of projects as each new aspect of the technique is introduced. The projects purposely start out simple and get a little more complex with each following chapter. You can choose to make any or all of them, but if you approach this book like a class (and make a small sampling of the projects) by the time "class" is over, you will have the knowledge to go on and crochet just about whatever you want.

So go ahead and get started. With a little time and patience, you will be amazed at your results.

A Trip To the Yarn Store

A trip to the yarn store can be as overwhelming as it is wonderful. If this is new territory for you, it's hard to know where to look first. Don't be intimidated by the dizzying array of colors and textures. Instead, embrace all the fabulous choices.

Plan to shop for yarn when you can take your time, look at everything, and then narrow down your selections and focus on them. Unless you know exactly what you need, never assume

that you can just run in and pick up some yarn. It just doesn't work that way. After all, choosing yarn is one of the most exciting parts of project planning.

The first yarn you will need is one to learn and practice on. Choose a yarn that is

- 〜 medium weight, such as DK or worsted (read on for an explanation);
- 〜 a light to medium color (it's difficult to see your stitches in a dark color); and
- 〜 smooth in texture.

Of course, when you are choosing yarn for a particular project, things get somewhat more specific. Yarn is divided into groups by weight. This weight is determined by the thickness of the yarn. Within each of those groups, the texture and content of the yarn can vary widely.

Within the last few years, the yarn industry has developed a system that assigns a number, called a CYCA classification, to each yarn to designate which category it falls into. There are six numbered categories, ranging from super fine to super bulky (see below). A symbol with the designated number appears on many yarn bands (it's a new system, so not all yarn companies are using it yet), as well as in published pattern instructions to help you match up appropriate yarns to patterns. This number will be your guideline, but a knowledgeable sales person can help you confirm your choice.

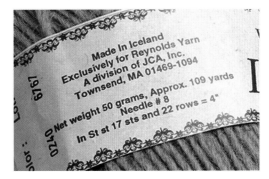

Yarn Label

STANDARD YARN WEIGHT SYSTEM						
YARN WEIGHT SYMBOL AND CATEGORY NAMES	**1** SUPER FINE	**2** FINE	**3** LIGHT	**4** MEDIUM	**5** BULKY	**6** SUPER BULKY
TYPE OF YARNS IN CATEGORY	Sock, Fingering, Baby	Sport, Baby	DK, Light Worsted	Worsted, Afghan, Aran	Chunky, Craft, Rug	Bulky, Roving
CROCHET GAUGE* RANGES IN SINGLE CROCHET TO 4 INCHES	21–32 sts	16–20 sts	12–17 sts	11–14 sts	8–11 sts	5–9 sts
RECOMMENDED HOOK IN METRIC SIZE RANGE	2.25–3.5mm	3.5–4.5mm	4.5–5.5mm	5.5–6.5mm	6.5–9mm	9mm and larger
RECOMMENDED HOOK IN U.S. SIZE RANGE	B-1 to E-4	E-4 to 7	7 to I-9	I-9 to K-10½	K-10½ to M-13	M-13 and larger
* GUIDELINES ONLY: The above reflect the most commonly used gauges and needle or hook sizes for specific yarn categories						

What About the Fiber Content?

In truth, you can crochet with any material that will go around your hook—from wire to string to the softest cashmere. Some fibers are easier to work with than others and will provide better results as a crocheted fabric. Smooth textures are the easiest to work with, but you are by no means limited to these. Yarns that are very bumpy are difficult to crochet with, due to the way stitches are formed. You may want to experiment with these yarns after you have a few projects under your belt.

For your first few projects, avoid yarns that are overly fuzzy, such as mohair, chenille, and eyelash. These yarns make it difficult to see your stitches and are hard to rip out if you make a mistake. That said, choose something you love and will enjoy working with, as you will be closely involved with it for the duration of your project!

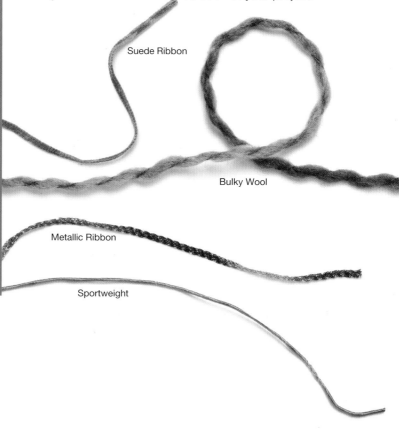

Worsted-weight Cotton

Suede Ribbon

Bulky Wool

Metallic Ribbon

Sportweight

Wool: Consider wool for warmth and softness—and the fact that it is springy: pull it and it will snap back into shape. This property makes it an ideal choice for clothing.

Cotton and linen: Cotton and linen have very little stretch, making them ideal for firmer pieces as well as open and lacy stitches. Try these yarns in everything from bags and baskets to heirloom table-cloths and bedspreads.

Silk and rayon: Two yarns above all others, silk and rayon, are known for their drape. They lend themselves well to dramatic shawls and scarves.

The end use of your project will also be a determining factor in your choice of fiber content. If you are making something for a child and need to consider practical matters, such as machine washability, you may want to use a machine-washable wool or a synthetic, such as an acrylic. Teens love bright, trendy colors, so if you're making something for a high-school-age niece, you may want to use a novelty yarn, such as ribbon. These yarns are often made out of synthetics, such as nylon or polyester, and create beautiful softness and drape at a reasonable price. Otherwise, natural fibers, such as cotton, rayon, wool, silk, and linen, will provide superior results.

In addition, there are many blends of naturals and synthetics that combine the best of both worlds. Some stores will allow you swatch (try out a yarn to make a small sample) before you buy, which is worth inquiring about. Many yarns look very different in the skein than they do when they are worked up. Sometimes, the same yarn can look stiff in single crochet and elegant in double crochet. Often, it's impossible to tell what a yarn will do until you work with it. This can be frustrating at times, but you'll also experience the ultimate thrill of discovery when it all falls together.

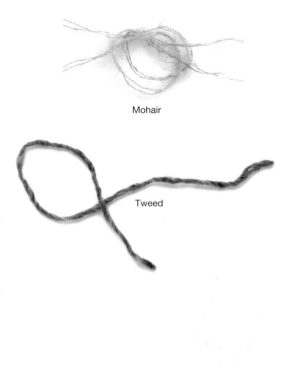

Mohair

Tweed

Your crochet hook is the next most important element. Hooks come in a variety of materials from aluminum to wood to bamboo, from acrylic to abalone to hand-forged brass. Personal preference dictates which material to use. Try several until you find the ones that feel comfortable in your hand.

Hook size is a little confusing as there are two separate numbering systems commonly used in the United States. The hooks we will be using in this book fall into the more common range. They are typically made of aluminum or plastic. They range in size from the smallest, B/1 (2.25 mm), to the largest, K/10½ (6.5 mm), and then move into plastic and up to a jumbo size S!

HOW DO I CHOOSE A CROCHET HOOK?
Hook size is a little confusing as there are two separate numbering systems commonly used in the United States.

The other range of hooks is referred to as steel crochet hooks, most commonly used for lace and fine work. This range starts with 00 (3.5 mm), which is the largest steel hook and about the same size as an E/4 (3.5 mm) in the aforementioned range. The hooks continue to get smaller in size as the numbers increase. Size 14 (0.75 mm), the smallest, resembles a bent pin!

For our purposes, assume that we are using a hook in the more common range unless the pattern specifically states steel. Also, as you become familiar with yarn weights and gauges, common sense will tell you to which range the pattern refers to.

Choosing Your First Hook

Along with your practice yarn, you'll need a hook to work with. Take another look at the yarn classification chart (page 9). You'll note that it also indicates the average hook size for each weight of yarn. This is really only a guideline; there are many variables involved in determining what size crochet hook to use. Factors determining correct hook size include

- your own personal crochet tension;
- the pattern stitch used in the project; and
- the end use of the project.

For example, if you are making a scarf, you'll want it to drape well and feel fluid as it wraps around your neck. To accomplish this, you'll likely use a larger hook than the one suggested by the guideline. If you are making a bag and want a sturdy fabric, you will probably need a smaller hook to give the fabric more body.

For practice, try a medium-sized crochet hook—either a size G/6 (4 mm), H/8 (5 mm), or I/9 (5.5 mm)—with your practice yarn.

Beyond your yarn and hook, you need surprisingly little additional equipment. This makes crochet an extremely portable hobby! Essential items include the following:

- A tape measure
- A small, sharp pair of scissors for trimming and snipping ends. Designate these "for crocheting use only"; using them to cut paper will dull them quickly.
- Open coil stitch markers. These very helpful tools allow you to mark a designated spot in your work but are easily removed without damaging your work. In a pinch you can substitute safety pins or even a paper clip.
- A yarn needle, preferably a few in different sizes. A yarn needle is a blunt-pointed needle with a large eye through which most yarns will fit.
- A knit-check. This metal ruler includes graduated holes to measure hook diameter and a window to easily measure gauge.

Of course, it's always nice to have a special tote bag to store your work in and a little bag for your equipment. Keep a notebook and a pencil handy to jot down notes or to keep track of your pattern as you work.

Other equipment can be added to your collection later, but for now, this is all you really need to get started crocheting.

WHAT ELSE DO I NEED?

Tape Measure

Scissors

Open Coil Stitch Markers

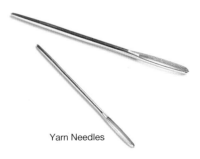

Yarn Needles

Gauge Ruler

2 Learning the Language

There is a certain jargon associated with crochet. As a beginner, don't be put off by terminology you don't understand. In this chapter, I will explain all the words and how crocheters abbreviate them. In a short time it will all make sense— you'll see.

To help you understand the terms and the flow of instructions, I will write out the pattern instructions using no crochet abbreviations for the first few chapters. As you become more familiar with the technique, I will abbreviate the basic terms. By the end of the book, you'll be up to speed with the standard way patterns are written.

Almost any pattern book or magazine will have a list of abbreviations used throughout the publication. If a given pattern contains abbreviations peculiar to that pattern, those abbreviations will be listed at the beginning of the pattern.

For this book, I will divide the most common terms and abbreviations into three categories: stitch words, direction words, and combinations and symbols. An alphabetized list of common crochet abbreviations also appears at the end of this chapter for handy reference.

Stitch Words

- All crochet begins with a **slipknot.** A slipknot is simply a knot that is adjustable.
- From a slipknot you create a **chain (ch),** which is the basis for all other stitches. A chain is also referred to as a **foundation chain** or a **beginning chain.**
- **Single crochet (sc)** is the most basic **stitch (st)** that is worked back into your foundation chain.
- **Half double crochet (hdc)** is a slightly longer stitch than single crochet.
- **Double crochet (dc)** is a longer stitch than single crochet or half double crochet.
- **Treble crochet (tr)** is longer yet, the longest of the basic stitches.
- A **slip stitch (sl st)** is used to join stitches, especially when working in **rounds (rnd[s])** or when working across existing stitches without adding more rows.
- All of these stitches are made up of **loops (lp[s]).**

A CLOSER LOOK AT ABBREVIATIONS

Let's go in a logical order. Remember, you're just looking at terms here. I'll explain how to make the stitches in the next chapter, "Putting It All Together."

Directions

Other terms you will encounter refer to what you will do with these stitches. For example, you will need to know the following:

- A pattern **begins (beg)** at the **beginning.**
- You may be asked to **continue (cont)** with a certain stitch or pattern.
- Sometimes a direction may apply only to **alternate (alt)** stitches or rows.
- A direction may take place on **following (foll)** rows.
- Often you will **repeat (rep)** a direction.
- This will result in the creation of a **pattern (patt)** stitch.
- As you encounter more complex pattern stitches you may be asked to **skip (sk)** a certain number of stitches.
- This will result in **spaces (sp[s]).**
- Sometimes you'll have a number of stitches **remaining (rem).**
- You may be asked to **yarn over (yo),** which means taking the yarn over the hook.

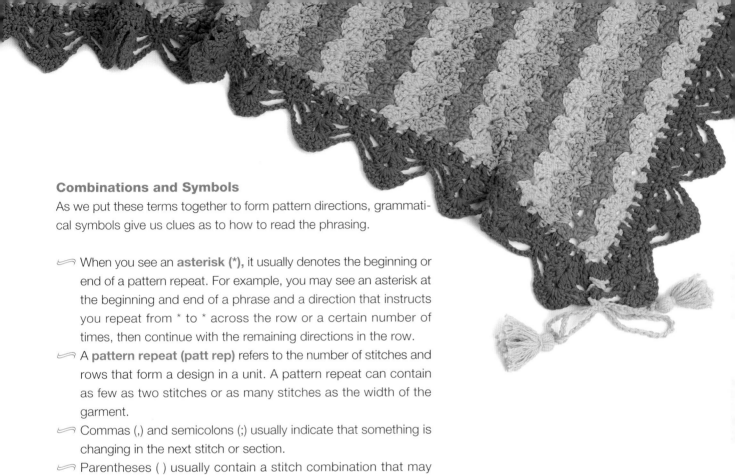

Combinations and Symbols

As we put these terms together to form pattern directions, grammatical symbols give us clues as to how to read the phrasing.

- When you see an **asterisk (*),** it usually denotes the beginning or end of a pattern repeat. For example, you may see an asterisk at the beginning and end of a phrase and a direction that instructs you repeat from * to * across the row or a certain number of times, then continue with the remaining directions in the row.
- A **pattern repeat (patt rep)** refers to the number of stitches and rows that form a design in a unit. A pattern repeat can contain as few as two stitches or as many stitches as the width of the garment.
- Commas (,) and semicolons (;) usually indicate that something is changing in the next stitch or section.
- Parentheses ( ) usually contain a stitch combination that may be repeated within a larger repeat or other information such as sizes.
- Brackets [ ] are used inside parentheses when a smaller section is repeated within a larger instruction.
- A period (.) is normally used at the end of a row or round. Think of each row or round as a complete sentence. When you see the period, the instructions for that row or round are finished.

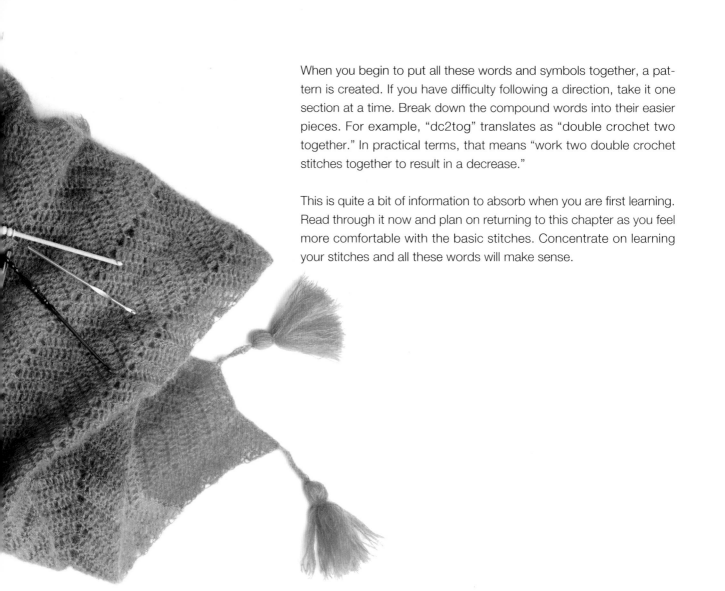

When you begin to put all these words and symbols together, a pattern is created. If you have difficulty following a direction, take it one section at a time. Break down the compound words into their easier pieces. For example, "dc2tog" translates as "double crochet two together." In practical terms, that means "work two double crochet stitches together to result in a decrease."

This is quite a bit of information to absorb when you are first learning. Read through it now and plan on returning to this chapter as you feel more comfortable with the basic stitches. Concentrate on learning your stitches and all these words will make sense.

Abbreviations

beg	begin(s); beginning	**rep**	repeat; repeating
bet	between	**rev sc**	reverse single crochet
CC	contrasting color	**rnd(s)**	round(s)
ch	chain	**RS**	right side
cm	centimeter(s)	**sc**	single crochet
cont	continue(s); continuing	**sl**	slip
dc	double crochet	**sl st**	slip(ped) stitch
dec(s)('d)	decrease(s); decreasing; decreased	**sp(s)**	space(es)
est	established	**st(s)**	stitch(es)
foll	follow(s); following	**tog**	together
g	gram(s)	**tr**	treble crochet
hdc	half double crochet	**WS**	wrong side
inc(s)('d)	increase(s); increasing; increased	**yd**	yard
MC	main color	**yo**	yarnover
m	marker	*****	repeat starting point
mm	millimeter(s)	*** ***	repeat all instructions between asterisks
patt(s)	pattern(s)	**( )**	alternate measurements and/or instructions
pm	place marker		
rem	remain(s); remaining	**[ ]**	work bracketed instructions a specified number of times

3 Putting It All Together

Learning to crochet is easier when you understand the theory behind it. In some ways, crochet is very similar to other yarn crafts, like knitting; but in other ways, it is very different. In this chapter, I'll show you how crochet works and explain the basic stitches.

Crochet is simply a fabric formed by a series of interlocking loops. A hook is used to create these loops, pulling one loop through another to create stitches. Unlike knitting (which is also a fabric created from interlocking loops but which uses two needles on which a number of open loops exist), crochet is created one stitch at a time. A new stitch is started after the previous one is completed.

Crochet is relatively easy to learn because each stitch builds on the knowledge of the previous stitch learned. That is to say, half double crochet is an expanded version of single crochet, and double crochet expands on it even more, and so on.

Now that you understand the theory, it's time to put it into practice. Let's learn some stitches!

The first thing you need to do is get comfortable holding the hook and yarn in your hands. There are two ways of holding the crochet hook: pencil style (Figure 1) or knife style (Figure 2). Try them both to see which way feels more comfortable to you.

Right-handed people usually hold the hook in their right hand; left-handed people in their left hand. Remember, crochet is found in so many different cultures that there are bound to be variations in hand position. There are certainly more "right" ways than "wrong" ways to hold the hook. It's not uncommon to feel awkward in the beginning, but with practice, your hands will feel more comfortable.

Equally important as how to hold the hook is how to hold the yarn (Figure 3). The yarn is held in the left hand (for right-handed people) and it is held "under tension." That means the yarn should be tight enough that you can easily grab it with the crochet hook but loose enough to slide through your fingers and let the hook slide back through the stitch. Holding the yarn under tension is very important, as it makes it easier to form stitches and is crucial to producing even stitches.

To hold the yarn under tension requires a system of wrapping the yarn in the hand opposite the crochet hook. Try wrapping the yarn around your index finger and, if it is comfortable, around your little finger as well. In addition, your thumb and middle finger hold the base of your work or the stitch you are working into. There are many ways to hold the yarn, so if this method isn't comfortable for you, try other arrangements until you find the perfect system for you.

HOLDING THE HOOK AND YARN

Figure 1

Figure 2

Figure 3

GETTING STARTED

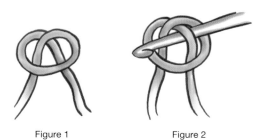

Figure 1   Figure 2

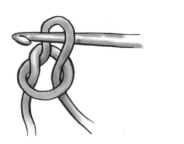

Figure 3

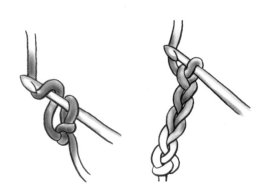

Figure 1   Figure 2

There are three things you'll need to know how to do to start any crochet project: making a slipknot, creating a foundation chain from chain stitches, and adding a turning chain.

Slipknot

As previously stated, crochet at its most basic definition is a series of loops. A stitch is made by pulling one loop through another loop. But somewhere there has to be a starting loop. That's where the slipknot comes in.

The slipknot is the first loop that goes on your hook. It does not count as a chain when you are counting chains or as a stitch in the first row worked. It is formed by hand out of two loops and it is an adjustable knot.

Starting about four to six inches (10 to 15 cm) from the end of the yarn, make a loop (Figure 1), insert the hook through the loop (Figure 2), and gently pull the end to tighten the loop on the hook (Figure 3). Don't pull the end too tightly or you won't be able to work into this stitch.

Chain Stitch

The first row of any crochet pattern—often called the foundation chain or row—is made using chain stitch. Holding the yarn as shown (Figure 3, page 21) in either your right or left hand, insert the hook under then over the yarn on your index finger (Figure 1) and pull the yarn through the loop on your hook. Repeat this step, moving your thumb and forefinger "up" the chain as you work, until the chain is the instructed length (Figure 2). Each loop counts as a stitch, except the loop on the hook.

Your turn: For your first practice piece, chain 21. That will give you one turning chain (more on turning chains below) and 20 stitches to work with.

Turning Chain

The turning chain is the number of chain stitches worked at the end or beginning of the row to achieve the required height for the next row of stitches (Figure 1). For single crochet, chain one extra stitch; for half double crochet, chain two extra stitches; for double crochet, chain three extra stitches; for treble crochet, chain four extra stitches.

4 3   2 1

Figure 1

In this book, the turning chain is made at the beginning of the row after the work is turned. While it is also acceptable to work the turning chain at the end of the row, *before* turning the work, the object here is to select one method and use it consistently throughout the projects unless the instructions specify otherwise.

However, the most important thing to remember about your turning chain is when it does or does not count as a stitch. Often a pattern will provide this information, but the rule to remember is that as your turning chain lengthens it is more likely to substitute for a stitch at the beginning of a row or round. Therefore, when working in single crochet and half double crochet your turning chain is just a vehicle to get you to the height of your new row and allow you wiggle room to work into the edge stitch on a row: it does not count as a stitch. Without a turning chain your work will become narrower with each row.

Your turn: Take a look at the chain you just made. Twenty of those chain stitches form the foundation chain for your work. The last chain, the one directly below the hook, is your turning chain. Watch how it comes into play in the next practice row.

THE STITCHES

In this book, we'll use four basic stitches to create the projects: single crochet, half double crochet, double crochet, and treble crochet. One thing to remember is the longer the stitch, the looser and more draped the resulting fabric will be. Therefore, single crochet is a dense, sturdy stitch, while treble crochet is more delicate and fluid.

Figure 1

Figure 2

Working Stitches

The most common way to hold the chain is with the loops (smooth side) facing you and inserting the hook under both the front and back loops of the chain (a). When you begin working the basic stitches, some patterns may call for you to work into only the front or back loop or around the post, the vertical bar of the stitch (b).

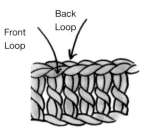

(a) The most common way to hold the chain is with the loops (smooth side) facing you.

(b) Some patterns may call for you to work into only the front or back loop or around the post.

Single Crochet

Make the foundation chain to the instructed length. Then begin the first row:

Step 1: Insert the hook through the second chain from the hook. The skipped chain is counted as a turning chain and is for height only; it does not count as a stitch (Figure 1).

Step 2: Take the yarn over the hook, and bring up a loop through chain (Figure 2).

Step 3: Yarn over hook again (Figure 3).

Step 4: Draw yarn through both loops on hook. This completes one single crochet (Figure 4).

Insert the hook into the next chain and repeat from the second step until the row is complete.

Step 5: At the end of the row, turn work to begin the next row. Chain one turning chain for height only, not counted as a stitch (Figure 5).

Step 6: Insert the hook under both top loops of the first single crochet, and beginning from the second step, continue to work one single crochet into each stitch across the row (Figure 6).

All following rows in single crochet are the same as this row.

Your turn: Use the foundation chain you created earlier as the base for a row of single crochet. See how the turning chain provides the height for the row of single crochet and helps you maintain straight edges on each side of your work? Read the section on the next page, "How to Work Rows," then add another couple rows of single crochet. Don't forget to add one turning chain at the beginning of each new row of single crochet.

Figure 3

Figure 4

Figure 5

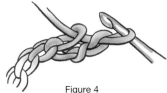

Figure 6

Figure 1

Figure 2

Figure 3

For the first row after the foundation chain is made, make one single crochet in each chain, starting with the second chain from the hook (the skipped chain acts as the turning chain). When you get to the end of the chain, turn the work around so that you are again working from right to left, chain 1. After working the foundation chain row, insert the hook under both halves of the crochet stitch (whatever crochet stitch is designated in the instructions) on subsequent rows.

The biggest challenge when you are beginning is keeping the stitch count constant. Missing a stitch, either at the beginning of a row or at the end of a row, is a very common error. Therefore, it's essential to count your stitches as you go until you are comfortable maintaining a constant stitch count. After that, count every several rows just to be sure you are on track.

Half Double Crochet

Make the foundation chain to the instructed length. Then begin the first row:

Step 1: With yarn over hook, insert the hook through the third chain from the hook. The two skipped chains are the turning chain, for height only (Figure 1).

Step 2: Take the yarn over the hook, and bring up a loop through the chain—three loops now on the hook (Figure 2).

Step 3: Yarn over hook again (Figure 3).

Step 4: Draw yarn through all three loops on hook. This completes one half double crochet. Yarn over hook, insert the hook into the next chain and repeat from the second step until the row is complete (Figure 4).

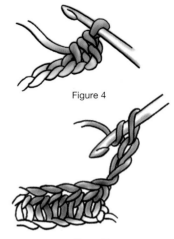

Figure 4

Step 5: At end of row, turn work to begin next row. Chain two—turning chain, does not count as stitch (Figure 5).

Step 6: Yarn over hook, and insert the hook under both top loops of the first half double crochet, and beginning from the second step, continue to work one half double crochet into each half double crochet across the row. Don't work into the turning chain of the previous row, or you'll gain a stitch (Figure 6).

Figure 5

All following rows in half double crochet are worked the same as this row.

Your turn: Continuing on with the piece of fabric you are creating, add a row or two of half double crochet to the last row of single crochet. Remember, you'll need to crochet two chains (turning chain) before you start each new row of half double crochet.

Figure 6

Figure 1   Figure 2

Figure 3   Figure 4

Figure 5   Figure 6

Double Crochet

Make the foundation chain to the instructed length. Then begin the first row:

Step 1: With yarn over hook, insert the hook through the fourth chain from the hook—the three skipped chains count as turning chain (Figure 1).

Step 2: Take the yarn over the hook, and bring through the chain—three loops are now on hook (Figure 2).

Step 3: Yarn over hook again (Figure 3).

Step 4: Draw yarn through first two loops on hook (Figure 4).

Step 5: Yarn over hook and draw yarn through remaining two loops. This completes one double crochet (Figure 5).

Yarn over hook, insert the hook into the next chain and repeat from the second step until the row is complete. Turn the work. Chain three for the turning chain to begin next row. The turning chain counts as the first double crochet of the next row.

Step 6: Yarn over hook, skip the first stitch, and insert the hook under both top loops of the next double crochet, and beginning from the second step, continue to work one double crochet into each stitch across the row (Figure 6).

All following rows of double crochet are done the same as this row.

Your turn: Continuing on with your practice piece, add a row or two of double crochet to the last row of half double crochet. You'll need three turning chains at the beginning of the row to equal the height of the row of double crochet.

Treble Crochet

Make the foundation chain to the instructed length. Then begin the first row:

Step 1: Wrap the yarn over hook twice, insert the hook through the fifth chain from the hook—the four skipped chains count as the turning chain (Figure 1).

Step 2: Take the yarn over the hook, and bring new yarn through the chain—four loops are now on hook (Figure 2).

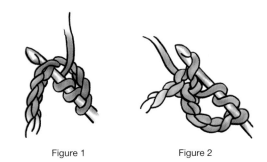

Figure 1   Figure 2

Step 3: Yarn over hook again and draw yarn through first two loops on hook—three loops are now on hook (Figure 3).

Step 4: Yarn over hook and draw yarn through next two loops on hook—two loops remain (Figure 4).

Figure 3   Figure 4

Step 5: Yarn over hook and draw yarn through last two loops on hook. This completes one treble crochet (Figure 5).

Yarn over hook twice, insert the hook into the next chain, and repeat from the second step until the row is complete. Turn the work at the end of the row. Chain four for the turning chain, and begin next row. The turning chain counts as the first treble crochet of the next row.

Step 6: Yarn over hook twice, skip the first stitch, and insert the hook under both top loops of the next treble crochet, and beginning from the second step, continue to work one treble crochet into each stitch across the row (Figure 6).

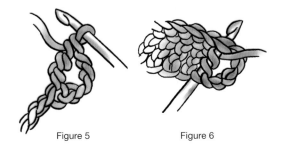

Figure 5   Figure 6

All following rows of treble crochet are worked the same as this row.

Your turn: Add a row or two of treble crochet to the last row of double crochet on your practice fabric. This time, you'll need four turning chains before you start each new row of treble crochet.

THE OTHER ELEMENTS

There are a few other crocheting techniques you'll need to know before you can make a crocheted project. Let's take a look at slip stitch, increasing, decreasing, joining new yarn, and working in rounds.

Slip Stitch

Make the foundation chain to the instructed length. Then begin the first row:

Figure 1

Insert the hook into the second chain from the hook, yarn over hook, and pull a loop through the stitch and the loop on the hook. One slip stitch has been worked. Insert the hook through the next chain and draw the loop through the chain and the loop on the hook. Continue to work a slip stitch across the row (see Figure 1). This makes a nice cord or edging. In this book, slip stitch is also used to join together two pieces of crocheted fabric or to move the yarn across other stitches without adding height or rows. When you work across other stitches, don't make a turning chain at the beginning of the slip stitches; wait until after the slip stitches are completed.

Your turn: Create an edging on your practice piece using slip stitch. There is no turning chain needed.

Work Even

When you see the instruction to "work even" in a pattern, simply continue on with the same number of stitches for the number of rows noted.

Increasing

To increase is to add one or more stitches. External increases are worked at the beginning or end of a row. Internal increases are worked within a row. Instructions are given in the patterns for each particular stitch being worked.

External: At the end of the previous row, work one additional chain stitch for each stitch to be increased, plus the number of turning chains. Turn work. Work the pattern stitch into the extra chain stitches and complete the row as usual (Figure 1).

Figure 1

Internal: The simplest way to increase is to work two stitches into one stitch (Figure 2).

Decreasing

To decrease is to eliminate one or more stitches. Internal decreases are worked within a row. External decreases are worked at the beginning or end of a row. Instructions are given in the patterns for each particular stitch being worked.

Figure 2

Method I: Simply skip a stitch, working into the second stitch, rather than the next one (Figure 1).

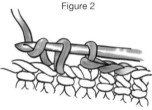

Method I, Figure 1

Method II: Draw a loop through each of the next two stitches, yarn over (Figure 1). Draw the yarn through all three loops on the hook. One stitch has been made from the two stitches (Figure 2).

Method II, Figure 1

Method II, Figure 2

Figure 1

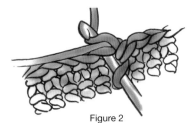

Figure 2

Figure 3

Joining a New Yarn

When making a project that requires more than one ball of yarn or more than one color, you will need to join a new yarn. Joining a new yarn is done either at the beginning of a row or, if working in a color pattern, while working a row. Do not knot the yarns in your work.

Beginning of row: Fasten off the old yarn. Attach the new yarn with a slipknot to the hook and start the row with the new yarn (Figure 1). Continue working as usual.

While working a row: Place the new yarn along the top of the work and crochet a few stitches over the new with the old yarn (Figure 2).

Change to the new yarn and begin working stitches with the new yarn over the old yarn (Figure 3).

After finishing the piece, work the ends into the wrong side of work.

Changing Colors

The technique for changing colors is easy. Cut the end of the color you are discontinuing, leaving a 6" (15 cm) tail. Begin working the new color in the next stitch, holding both the cut end and the new end taut in your opposite hand and laying both ends over the top of the stitches to be worked. Continue working the pattern as established for several stitches; the ends will lie on top of the work and you will crochet over them with the new yarn as you work into each stitch (Figure 1). Once the new yarn is secure, release the ends, but work a few more stitches over them. Trim ends and continue working the new yarn.

Figure 1

Working in Rounds

Many patterns start with a foundation chain with a specified number of stitches where the last chain is joined to the first chain with a slip stitch, forming a circle. This is called crocheting in rounds. When crocheting in rounds you are usually working on the right side of the work only, with no turning.

Version I:

Step 1: Chain the required number of stitches and join with a slip stitch to form a ring (Figure 1).

Step 2: The pattern will then start reading "rounds" instead of "rows." You will work the pattern stitch into each chain stitch as you would a row, and when you come back to the starting place, a round has been completed. Join with a slip stitch to the first stitch. The pattern instructions may tell you to work the new stitches into the ring; this means you work the stitches over the chains instead of into them (Figure 2).

Version II:

Step 1: Wrap yarn around your index finger three times (Figure 1).

Step 2: Place hook over the end of yarn attached to yarn ball (Figure 2).

Version I, Figure 1

Version I, Figure 2

Version II, Figure 1

Version II, Figure 2

Figure 3

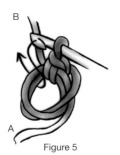

Figure 4

Step 3: Yarn over and pull through loop on hook (Figure 3).

Steps 4 and 5: Continue working single crochet around the two strands until required number of stitches (Figures 4 and 5).

Step 6: Pull yarn end slightly (Figure 6).

Step 7: Pull yarn A, then pull yarn B and tighten yarn B (Figure 7).

Step 8: Tighten yarn A by pulling the end (Figure 8).

Step 9: Join with slip stitch to the first stitch (Figure 9).

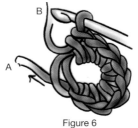

Figure 5

Figure 6

Figure 7

Figure 8

Figure 9

After you understand stitches and how to make them, the next most important concept to understand in order to create beautiful garments that fit is that of gauge. Gauge (sometimes referred to as tension) is simply your number of stitches and rows per inch. (Figures 1 and 2)

Each pattern is written to a specific gauge determined by the designer. The designer bases these calculations on the assumption that when you are making this pattern your gauge will be the same as that stated on the pattern.

However, because this is work being created by human hands and not machines, there are many factors that can affect gauge. Therefore, even if you are using the exact same yarn listed on the pattern, you still need to make a gauge swatch.

To make a gauge swatch, consult your pattern for the number of stitches the gauge is being measured over and the recommended hook size. The pattern should also state what stitch was used for the swatch. It will read something like "18 stitches and 18 rows = 4" (10 cm) in single crochet with a size H/8 (5 mm) hook."

For that pattern, you'd need to chain enough for at least 18 stitches plus the turning chain, but preferably more. Work in the stated stitch to a total length of at least 4" (10 cm). Lay your swatch on a flat surface, and using a ruler (as opposed to a tape measure) or a knit check, measure the number of stitches within 1" (cm) and also within 4" (10 cm). Repeat the same procedure for rows.

If you are unsure of the gauge, measure in a few different places. If you have more stitches than the pattern calls for, you are crocheting too tight and need to use a larger hook. If you have fewer stitches, you are crocheting too loose and need to use a smaller hook. Repeat the swatch until your measurements agree with the pattern. It is important to be as exact as possible. What seems like a fraction of an inch (cm) difference on your swatch can result in a several-inch (-cm) difference on a garment.

GAUGE

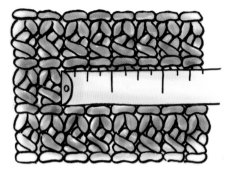

Figure 1

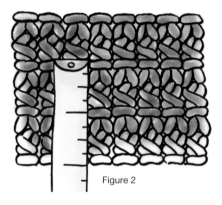

Figure 2

FINISHING TECHNIQUES

Once you've completed a piece, there are several things you'll need to know in order to finish it so you have a neat, tidy—and sturdy—end result. Let's take a look at how to weave in ends and block your finished piece.

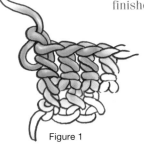

Figure 1

Figure 2

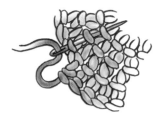

Figure 3

Weaving in Ends

Fastening Off: At the end of the last row, cut the yarn, leaving a 4" (10 cm) tail for weaving in. Insert the tail through the last stitch and pull to tighten and secure (Figure 1).

In Seam Allowances: When working in rows, weave the yarn ends into the seam allowances whenever possible. If there isn't a seam allowance, weave the ends into the wrong side of work catching the back side of the crochet stitch (Figure 2).

In Rounds: When working in rounds, weave the ends vertically into the back of the work (Figure 3).

Blocking

This process helps eliminate any unevenness from your crocheting, smoothes the seams, and sets the drape. There are two ways of blocking, either by steam or by wetting down the piece. You can block individual pieces before sewing them together or block the whole piece after it's assembled.

You'll need a few things to block your garment: a surface you can stick pins into, rustproof pins, a measuring device, and the finished dimensions of the piece. The surface can be as simple as a large towel spread out on a padded carpet or the top of your bed. The easiest pins to use are T-pins or pins with glass heads.

To use your steam iron for blocking, hold it a short distance above the crocheted piece to allow the steam to penetrate the fibers. Once you've steamed the surface, let it dry before removing the pins.

Wet blocking uses more moisture than steam blocking and can be used to stretch and enlarge a crocheted piece. Once you've pinned out the piece, use a spray-mist bottle with a fine, even mist. Gently pat the moisture into the piece. Again, let it dry before you remove the pins. During the blocking process—steam or wet—remember not to flatten any raised stitches.

4 Single Crochet

Now that you are familiar with the basic crochet stitches, let's put your knowledge to use. The projects in this chapter are simple . . . But, simple does not have to be boring!

Instead of using the same old yarn to make the same old scarf, I've chosen to use beautiful yarns that work up into even more beautiful fabrics. The finishing accents—like fringes and lettering—need only a simple stitch or two to show the projects off to their best advantage.

All of the projects in this chapter have two things in common: single crochet and rectangles. Why? Because using just one stitch—single crochet—and working that stitch into just one shape—a rectangle—allows you to focus on the basics. And the basics you'll want to master are these:

➥ Work to the gauge of the pattern
➥ Keep the stitch count constant

Mastering these two items will keep the edges of your pieces even and give you gorgeous finished projects.

What's the best way to master gauge and stitch count? Count as you go. Count every stitch for the first few rows; then count stitches on intermittent rows. Before you know it, you'll have a stunning finished project with a super-straight edge.

Let's get started!

Quintessential Scarf

Need to know

Gauge (page 35)

Slipknot (page 22)

Chain stitch (page 22)

Turning chain (page 23)

Single crochet (pages 24–25)

Fasten off (page 36)

Making fringe (page 39)

Weaving in loose ends
(page 36)

Blocking (page 36)

This easy-to-make scarf is a beginning crocheter's quintessential first project. A simple stitch shows off a beautiful yarn. A large hook keeps the look relaxed and produces rapid results.

No shaping or fitting is involved, and narrow rows make it easy to count stitches and keep them constant.

Finished Size

Width: 8" (20.5 cm)

Length: 65" (165 cm), excluding fringe

Materials

Yarn: CYCA classification: 5 Bulky; about 330 yards (302 meters).

Shown here: Tahki Soho (100% wool; 110 yards [100 meters], 100 grams): #333 chartreuse, 3 skeins.

Hook: Size M/13 (9 mm). Adjust hook size if necessary to obtain correct gauge.

Notions: Yarn needle, for working in ends; heavy cardboard about 3 × 5" (7.5 × 12.5 cm), for measuring fringe.

Gauge

9 single crochet = 4" (10 cm) and 8 rows = 3" (7.5 cm) with size M/13 (9 mm) hook.

Tip: Every row of this scarf has 18 single crochet. In order to keep the edges of your scarf straight, either count each single crochet as you make it or count the number of stitches in the entire row before you move on to the next row. Dropping or adding stitches will give your scarf an uneven edge.

Scarf

Using the hook size needed to obtain the correct gauge, loosely chain 19.

Row 1: Starting in second chain from hook, work 1 single crochet in each chain to end, turn work—18 single crochet.

Row 2: Chain 1, work 1 single crochet in each single crochet across the row, turn work.

Repeat Row 2 until work measures 65" (165 cm) long or desired length. Fasten off.

Finishing

Thread loose ends on the yarn needle, weave in ends, and trim excess. Cut 72 ten-inch (25.5 cm) strands of yarn and use cardboard as a measuring guide to make fringe (Figure 1). *Working along one short edge of the scarf and using 2 yarn strands at a time, fold strands in half and use crochet hook to pull folded end through *one* stitch (Figure 2). Insert hook through loop created by folded end, then pull strand ends through loop*. Repeat fringe instructions from * to * making a fringe in each stitch along the short edge of the scarf— 18 fringes. Work the same number of fringes across the other short edge of the scarf. When fringes are finished, trim fringe ends to even them, if necessary. Steam or block the scarf as needed.

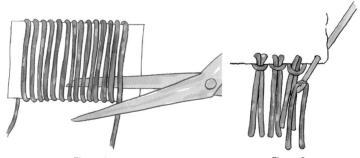

Figure 1   Figure 2

New Direction Scarf

Need to know

Gauge (page 35)

Slipknot (page 22)

Chain stitch (page 22)

Turning chain (page 23)

Single crochet (pages 24–25)

Stitch markers (page 13)

Fasten off (page 36)

Making fringe (page 39)

Weaving in loose ends
(page 36)

Blocking (page 36)

Take a bulky yarn with color interest of its own, find a large hook, work horizontally to show the coloration off to its best advantage, and you've got a scarf in no time! This is an excellent project to hone your beginning crochet skills, and the results are so beautiful that you'll want to share your creation with friends and family.

Finished Size

Width: 8" (20.5 cm)

Length: 72" (183 cm) long, excluding fringe

Materials

Yarn: CYCA classification: 5 Bulky; about 372 yards (340 meters).

Shown here: Reynolds Smile (72% acrylic, 28% wool; 124 yards [114 meters], 100 grams): #201 variegated mixture of charcoal/acid yellow/reds, 3 skeins.

Hook: Size N/15 (10 mm). Adjust hook size if necessary to obtain correct gauge.

Notions: Yarn needle, for working in ends; heavy cardboard about 3 × 5" (7.5 × 12.5 cm), for measuring fringe.

Gauge

8 single crochet and 9 rows = 4" (10 cm) with size N/15 (10 mm) hook.

Note: The scarf is made horizontally, meaning the stitches across the row comprise the scarf length and the rows form the width. Although each row is long, you won't have many of them to make!

Scarf

Using the hook size needed to obtain the correct gauge, loosely chain 145 stitches.

Row 1: Starting with second chain from hook, work 1 single crochet in each chain to end, turn work—144 single crochet.

Tip: Can't count to 144 without getting interrupted by someone or something? Try adding a stitch marker—a piece of yarn or a safety pin—every 20, 40, or 50 stitches to help you keep your place.

Row 2: Chain 1, work 1 single crochet in each single crochet, turn work.

Repeat Row 2 until scarf measures 8" (20.5 cm) wide or desired width (if you decide to make a longer or wider scarf, you'll need more yarn). Fasten off.

Finishing

Thread loose ends on yarn needle and weave in to secure; trim excess. Cut 96 ten-inch (25.5 cm) strands of yarn and use cardboard as a measuring guide to make fringe (Figure 1, page 39). *Working along one short edge of the scarf and using 3 yarn strands at a time, fold strands in half and use crochet hook to pull folded end through *one* stitch (Figure 2, page 39). Insert hook through loop created by folded end, then pull strand ends through loop*. Repeat fringe instructions from * to * making a fringe in each stitch along the short edge of the scarf—16 fringes. Work the same number of fringes across the other short edge of the scarf. When fringes are finished, trim fringe ends to even them, if necessary. Block or steam lightly as needed.

Striped Strip Pillow

Need to know
Gauge (page 35)
Slipknot (page 22)
Chain stitch (page 22)
Turning chain (page 23)
Single crochet (pages 24–25)
Fasten off (page 36)
Changing colors (page 32)
Slip stitch (page 30)
Making buttonholes (page 61)
Weaving in loose ends
(page 36)

Narrow strips crocheted with stripes then joined together add more interesting patterns, colors, and textures than just stripes alone. Working in single crochet keeps the technique simple. The stripe colors are accented on the flapped back of the pillow. Follow the sequence set for this pillow or create your own series of stripes. This is also a great way to use up some of those odd yarns from your stash—just make sure they are all the same gauge.

Finished Size
Front: 16 × 16" (40.5 × 40.5 cm)
Back: 15 × 15" (38 × 38 cm)
Note: The Front curves around the pillow edges slightly to meet the Back when the pillow form is inserted.

Materials
Yarn: CYCA classification: 4 Medium, Worsted Weight; about 300 yards (274.5 meters) of one main color and 100 yards (91.5 meters) each of 6 accent colors.

Shown here: Cascade Yarns Cascade 220 (100% wool; 220 yards [201 meters], 100 grams): #4002 charcoal (main color), 2 skeins; #7827 yellow (A), #7824 orange (B), #9404 dark red (C), #8229 sage (D), #2414 rust (E), #9421 turquoise (F), 1 skein each.

Hook: Size H/8 (5 mm). Adjust hook size if necessary to obtain correct gauge.

Notions: 6 buttons, about ⅞–1" (2.2–2.5 cm) in diameter; safety pins; yarn needle, for working in ends; 16" (40.5 cm) pillow form; sewing needle and thread, for basting.

Gauge
17 stitches and 19 rows = 4" (10 cm) with size H/8 (5 mm) hook in single crochet.

Pillow Front
Working in single crochet, make 5 panels following the stripe sequence listed on page 44. Each panel is 16 stitches wide and 72 rows long.

Pillow Front

Rows 1–2: Color A (yellow)

Rows 3–4: Color B (orange)

Rows 5–6: Color A

Rows 7–10: Color B

Rows 11–16: Color C (dark red)

Rows 17–18: Color D (sage)

Rows 19–20: Color C

Rows 21–24: Color D

Rows 25–26: Main Color (charcoal)

Rows 27–28: Color E (rust)

Rows 29–30: Main Color

Rows 31–34: Color E

Rows 35–36: Color F (turquoise)

Rows 37–38: Color E

Rows 39–44: Color F

Rows 45–46: Color D

Rows 47–48: Color F

Rows 49–50: Color D

Rows 51–52: Color A

Rows 53–54: Color D

Rows 55–58: Color A

Rows 59–60: Color B

Rows 61–62: Color A

Rows 63–64: Color C

Rows 65–70: Color B

Rows 71–72: Color C

Basic Pattern

Using hook size needed to obtain correct gauge and the designated color, loosely chain 17.

Row 1: Chain 1, beginning in second chain from hook, work 1 single crochet in each chain to end, turn work—16 single crochet.

Row 2: Chain 1, beginning in first single crochet, work 1 single crochet in each single crochet to end of row—16 stitches. Repeat Row 2 for pattern.

Panel 1: Work basic pattern as above for Rows 1–72 following the color stripe sequence.

Panel 2: Begin as first panel, working colors as stated in Rows 19–72, then work Rows 1–18.

Panel 3: Begin as first panel, working colors as stated in Rows 37–72, then work Rows 1–36.

Panel 4: Begin as first panel, working colors as stated in Rows 55–72, then work Rows 1–54.

Panel 5: Work same as first panel in colors stated for Rows 1–72.

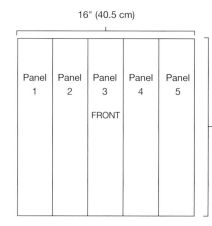

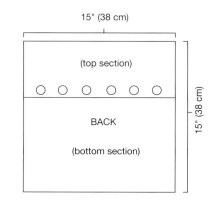

Pillow Back

The pillow back is made of 2 overlapping pieces. The bottom piece measures 15 × 10" (38 x 25.5 cm); the upper piece measures 15 × 6" (38 × 15 cm). The back is intentionally worked slightly smaller than the pillow front.

Bottom section

With main color, chain 66.

Row 1: Beginning in second chain from hook, work 1 single crochet in each chain to end, turn work—65 single crochet.

Row 2: Chain 1, beginning in first single crochet, work 1 single crochet in each stitch to end of row, turn work.

Repeat Row 2 until bottom section of back measures 10" (25.5 cm) from beginning. Fasten off main color.

Top section

With main color, chain 66.

Row 1: Beginning in second chain from hook, work 1 single crochet in each chain to end, turn work—65 single crochet.

Row 2: Chain 1, beginning in first single crochet, work 1 single crochet in each stitch to end of row.

Repeat Row 2 until top section measures 5½" (14 cm) from beginning chain. Fasten off main color. Continuing with top section, begin color section for buttonhole border as noted on page 46.

Pillow Back

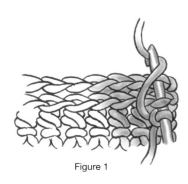

Figure 1

Figure 2

Row 1: Attach color C to last row of main color, chain 1, work 1 single crochet in each single crochet, turn work. Fasten off color C.

Row 2: Attach color E, chain 1, work 1 single crochet in each single crochet, turn work. Fasten off color E.

Row 3: Attach color D, chain 1, work 1 single crochet in each single crochet, turn work. Fasten off color D.

Row 4 (buttonholes): Attach color F, chain 1, *work 1 single crochet in each of first 6 single crochet, chain 4, skip next 4 single crochet*; repeat from * to * 5 more times, work 1 single crochet in each of last 5 single crochet, turn work. Fasten off color F.

Row 5: Attach color B, chain 1, work 1 single crochet in each of first 5 single crochet, *work 1 single crochet in each of next 4 chains, work 1 single crochet in each of next 6 single crochet*; repeat from * to * 5 more times, turn work. Fasten off color B.

Row 6: Attach A, chain 1, work 1 single crochet in each single crochet to end of row. Fasten off A.

Finishing

Using safety pins, pin together front panels in numerical order with wrong sides together. Join using single crochet and main color (Figures 1 and 2) so that seam appears on right side of work and edge stitch of panel forms seam allowance. Pin top of back to bottom of back, overlapping the top over the bottom to form a 15" (38 cm) square; with sewing needle and thread, baste side edges together to hold the 2 back pieces together. With wrong sides together, pin Front to Back of pillow, easing top slightly to fit. Using main color and beginning at any corner, chain 1; work 1 row single crochet evenly around outside edge, working through all thicknesses as needed, join to chain 1 with slip stitch at beginning of round, fasten off. Remove basting thread. Weave in loose ends. Sew buttons opposite buttonholes. Stuff pillow form into pillow cover, making sure to push form into corners; smooth out evenly. Front will curve over the pillow form edges slightly to meet Back.

Beaded D Ring Belt

Need to know
Gauge (page 35)
Slipknot (page 22)
Chain stitch (page 22)
Turning chain (page 23)
Single crochet (pages 24–25)
Fasten off (page 36)
Changing colors (page 32)
Weaving in loose ends (page 36)
Making fringe (page 39)

A belt is an easy way to make a fashion statement. A variety of beads dress up the fringe on this easily accomplished belt. It works up so quickly that you can easily make several, playing with colors and bead choices for varied effects. Slightly retro yet very up-to-date, the D ring closure allows for easy size adjustability.

Finished Size

Width: 2" (5 cm)

Length: 44" (112 cm), before attaching D rings

Materials

Yarn: CYCA classification: 4 Medium, Worsted Weight; about 40 yards (36.5 meters) each of colors A, B, and C.

Shown here: Classic Elite Yarns Bam Boo (100% bamboo; 77 yards [70 meters], 50 grams): #4985 orange (A), #4915 celery (B), #4971 fuchsia (C), 1 skein each.

Hook: Size H/8 (5 mm). Adjust hook size if necessary to obtain the correct gauge.

Notions: 1 set of D rings, 2" (5 cm) wide; about 46 assorted beads, with holes large enough to thread onto yarn, varying between e-beads and pony beads in size; yarn needle; sewing needle and thread; piece of cardboard about 3" (7.5 cm) square, to use for measuring fringe.

Gauge

16 single crochet and 16 rows = 4" (10 cm) with size H/8 (5 mm) hook.

Belt

Using the hook size needed to obtain the correct gauge and color A (orange), loosely chain 177.

Row 1: Starting with second chain from hook, work 1 single crochet in each chain to end, turn work—176 single crochet.

Row 2: Chain 1, work 1 single crochet in each single crochet. Fasten off A, leaving a 3" (7.5 cm) tail, turn work.

Row 3: Attach color C (fuchsia) by pulling up a loop in the end single crochet, leaving a 3" (7.5 cm) tail and working 1 chain to secure; work 1 single crochet in same stitch, then work 1 single crochet in each single crochet to end, turn work.

Row 4: Still using color C, repeat Row 2.

Row 5: With color B (celery), repeat Row 3.

Row 6: Still using color B, repeat Row 2.

Row 7: With color C, repeat Row 3.

Row 8: Still using color C, repeat Row 2.

Row 9: With A, repeat Row 3.

Row 10: Still using A, repeat Row 2. Fasten off, leaving a 3" (7.5 cm) tail.

Finishing

Attach D rings to end of belt without 3" (7.5 cm) yarn tails. Fold ¾" (2 cm) over the straight side of the D rings, and pin in place. Thread A on yarn needle and whipstitch folded end to belt (Figure 1). Remove pins. Cut twenty 6" (15 cm) strands of yarn using a combination of all three colors and use cardboard as a measuring guide to make fringe. Attach fringe to end of belt that has existing tails using 2 strands per stitch and mixing existing tails into fringe. Attach 1 bead to each piece of fringe by threading yarn tail on yarn needle and inserting needle through bead; remove yarn needle. Randomly mix bead styles as desired. Knot each fringe under each bead to hold beads in place.

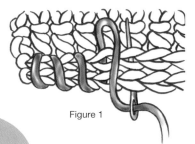

Figure 1

Single Crochet

Ribbed Tie Belt

Need to know

Gauge (page 35)

Slipknot (page 22)

Chain stitch (page 22)

Turning stitch (page 23)

Single crochet (pages 24–25)

Working through the back loop (below)

Fasten off (page 36)

Changing colors (page 32)

Weaving in loose ends (page 36)

Making fringe (page 39)

Adding beads (page 50)

This belt has one minor change from the D ring belt in the way the stitch is worked. Yet the effect makes it look totally different— more dimensional and more drape. Try making it as a wider sash for yet another look.

Finished Size

Width: 2" (5 cm)

Length: 56" (142 cm), excluding fringe

Materials

Yarn: CYCA classification: 4 Medium, Worsted Weight; about 77 yards (70.5 meters) each of colors A and B; about 40 yards (36.5 meters) each of colors C and D.

Shown here: Classic Elite Yarns Bam Boo (100 % bamboo; 77 yards [70 meters], 50 grams): #4954 raspberry (A), #4915 celery (B), #4985 orange (C), #4971 fuchsia (D); 1 skein each.

Hook: Size H/8 (5 mm). Adjust hook size if necessary to obtain the correct gauge.

Notions: Yarn needle; 12 assorted beads, about e-bead or pony bead size, in wood and gold tone; piece of sturdy cardboard about 4 × 6" (10 × 15 cm), for measuring fringe.

Gauge

16 single crochet and 16 rows = 4" (10 cm) with size H/8 (5 mm) hook.

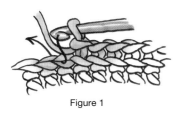

Figure 1

Belt

Using the hook size needed to obtain correct gauge and color A (raspberry), loosely chain 225.

Row 1: Beginning with second chain from hook, work 1 single crochet in each chain to end, turn work—224 single crochet.

Note: From this point onward, each single crochet in every row is worked through the back loop (Figure 1).

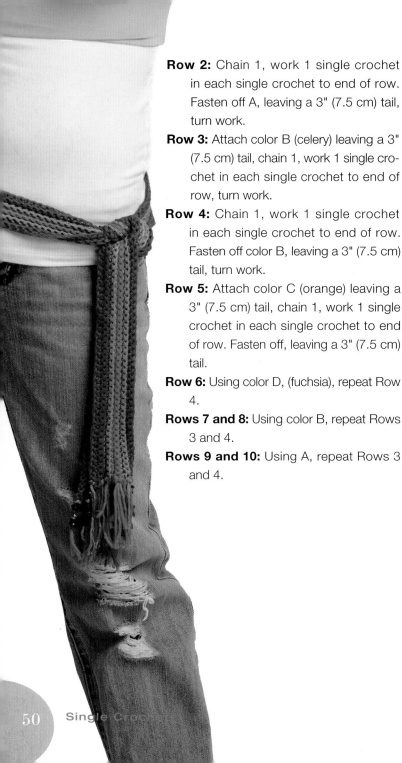

Row 2: Chain 1, work 1 single crochet in each single crochet to end of row. Fasten off A, leaving a 3" (7.5 cm) tail, turn work.

Row 3: Attach color B (celery) leaving a 3" (7.5 cm) tail, chain 1, work 1 single crochet in each single crochet to end of row, turn work.

Row 4: Chain 1, work 1 single crochet in each single crochet to end of row. Fasten off color B, leaving a 3" (7.5 cm) tail, turn work.

Row 5: Attach color C (orange) leaving a 3" (7.5 cm) tail, chain 1, work 1 single crochet in each single crochet to end of row. Fasten off, leaving a 3" (7.5 cm) tail.

Row 6: Using color D, (fuchsia), repeat Row 4.

Rows 7 and 8: Using color B, repeat Rows 3 and 4.

Rows 9 and 10: Using A, repeat Rows 3 and 4.

Finishing

Thread loose ends on the yarn needle, weave in ends, and trim excess. Cut 40 strands of yarn (10 strands of each color) about 6" (15 cm) in length and use cardboard as a measuring guide (Figure 1, page 39). You'll be supplementing the existing 3" (7.5 cm) yarn tails with the new fringes and using fringe strands only in stitches where the long yarn tails don't exist. *Working along one short edge of the scarf, using 2 yarn strands at a time, and mixing the colors together randomly, fold the strands in half and use crochet hook to pull folded end through *one* stitch (Figure 2, page 39). Insert hook through loop created by folded end; then pull strand ends through loop*. Repeat fringe instructions from * to * making a fringe in each stitch along the short edge of belt—10 fringes total. Work the same number of fringes across the other short edge of the belt. When fringes are finished, trim fringe ends to even them, if necessary.

Add beads

Thread yarn needle with last strand in the end fringe and insert needle through 3 beads, remove yarn needle, slide the beads up to the belt edge, then tie an overhand knot at the fringe edge to secure beads; separate the beads by tying an overhand knot between each bead. Work the beading process from * to * on both end strands at each belt end—12 beads total.

Handy Utility Cases

Need to know

Gauge (page 35)

Slipknot (page 22)

Chain stitch (page 22)

Turning stitch (page 23)

Single crochet (pages 24–25)

Single crochet through
  2 layers (page 46)

Slip stitch (page 30)

Fasten off (page 36)

Weaving in loose ends
  (page 36)

Blocking (page 36)

Cross-stitch (page 53)

Whipstitch (page 48)

Once you have mastered the scarf and the belt, which are just rectangular strips of crocheted fabric, the next step is to think about what kinds of crocheted items you can make by joining straight pieces. These handy little cases, designed to hold your cell phone and iPod music player, are quick to make. They require a little bit of construction, still done with crochet. Embroidery is only a suggestion. Keep them in your purse or tote or on yourself with the optional straps.

Finished Sizes

Cell Phone Case

Width: 3½" (9 cm)

Length: 6" (15 cm)

Music Player Case

Width: 3" (7.5 cm)

Length: 4½" (11.5 cm)

Materials

Yarn: CYCA classification: 2 Fine, Sportweight (used double); about 170 yards (186 meters) for cell phone case and about 100 yards (91.5 meters) for music player case, plus about 25 yards (23 meters) contrasting color for construction and embroidery for each.

Shown here: Jaeger's Trinity (40% silk, 35% cotton, 25% polyamide fiber; 218 yards [200 meters], 50 grams): #440 fuchsia (cell phone case), #438 denim (trim on cell phone case), 1 skein each; #436 chartreuse (music player case), #440 fuchsia (trim on music player case), 1 skein each.

Hook: Size G/6 (4 mm). Adjust hook size if necessary to obtain correct gauge.

Notions: Large snaps, size 4 (1 for each case); sewing needle and thread; safety pins; yarn needle for working in ends and embroidery; small piece of sew-on Velcro, for music player case; 1 set of D rings, ¾" (2 cm) wide (optional), for cell phone case.

Gauge

17 single crochet and 18 rows = 4" (10 cm) with size G/6 (4 mm) hook.

Cell Phone Case
Front
Using the hook size needed to obtain the correct gauge and fuchsia, loosely chain 16 stitches.

Row 1: Starting in second chain from hook, work 1 single crochet in each chain to end, turn work—15 single crochet.
Row 2: Chain 1, work 1 single crochet in each single crochet, turn work.

Repeat Row 2 until work measures a total length of 6" (15 cm). Fasten off.

Back
Work as for Front to a total length of 7½" (19 cm). The extra length will serve as the closing flap. If needed, smooth out both pieces with a light touch of steam. Allow to dry before continuing. Fasten off.

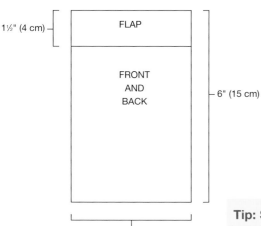

1½" (4 cm) — FLAP

FRONT
AND
BACK

6" (15 cm)

3½" (9 cm)

Tip: Simple embroidery is a great way to add a special touch to your finished crochet pieces. Use cross-stitch to make block letters.

Strap (optional)

With 2 strands of denim and same hook used for project, loosely chain 150. Work 1 slip stitch in each chain. Fasten off. Weave in loose ends. With 1 strand of yarn threaded on tapestry needle, attach 1 D ring at each upper side edge as shown in photo. Tie straps to D Ring using overhand knot.

Finishing

With a single strand of denim threaded in yarn needle and using cross-stitch, follow chart (Figure 1) to embroider "hello" on Front and Back, if desired. Each square represents one stitch. With yarn needle, weave in loose ends to wrong side of work. With wrong sides of work facing together (right sides facing out), pin Front to Back with safety pins, carefully matching side and lower edges. Beginning at upper corner of Front with same hook used for project and single strand of denim, work one row of single crochet evenly around side and bottom edges, working through both layers. Continue single crochet evenly around single layer of the remainder of back (to create flap), slip-stitch last stitch to beginning stitch and fasten off. With sewing needle and thread, sew snap to center of flap edge and upper edge of Front.

Cross-stitch

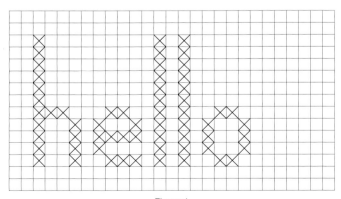

Figure 1

Music Player Case
Front
Using the hook size needed to obtain the correct gauge and 2 strands of chartreuse held together, loosely chain 14 stitches.

Row 1: Starting in second chain from hook, work 1 single crochet in each chain to end, turn work—13 single crochet.

Row 2: Chain 1, work 1 single crochet in each single crochet, turn work.

Repeat Row 2 until piece measures 4½" (11.5 cm). Fasten off.

Back
Work as for Front to a total length of 6" (15 cm). The extra length will serve as the closing flap. Fasten off. If needed, smooth out both pieces with a light touch of steam. Allow to dry before continuing.

1½" (3.8 cm) — FLAP

FRONT AND BACK

4½" (11.5 cm)

3" (9 cm)

Finishing

With single strand of fuchsia threaded on yarn needle and using cross-stitch, embroider "tunes" on Back following chart (Figure 2). Weave in loose ends on wrong side of work. With wrong sides together (right sides facing out), pin Front to Back with safety pins, carefully matching side and lower edges. Beginning at upper corner of Front with same hook used for project and single strand of fuchsia, work one row of single crochet evenly around side and bottom edges, working through both layers. Continue single crochet evenly around single layer of remainder of back (to create flap), slip-stitch last stitch to beginning stitch and fasten off. With sewing needle and thread, sew snap to center of flap edge and upper edge of Front.

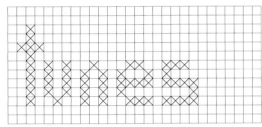

Figure 2

 1 single crochet stitch

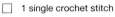 1 cross-stitch

Belt Loop (optional)

To make belt loop, with 2 strands of chartreuse and same size hook used for project, chain 6.

Row 1: Beginning in second chain from hook, work 1 single crochet in each chain to end, turn work—5 single crochet.

Row 2: Chain 1, work 1 single crochet in each single crochet, turn work.

Repeat Row 2 until belt loop measures 3" (7.5 cm) from beginning. Fasten off.

Place the top edge of loop about ¾" (2 cm) down from the folded top edge of case and about ⅜" (1 cm) from right-hand case edge. Pin belt loop in place. Using 1 strand of chartreuse threaded on yarn needle, whipstitch the top of belt loop to the case back. Sew ¾" (2 cm) square of Velcro at lower edge of loop and to corresponding spot on back of case.

Glamour Girl Cosmetic Bag

Need to know

Gauge (page 35)

Slipknot (page 22)

Chain stitch (page 22)

Turning chain (page 23)

Single crochet (pages 24–25)

Backstitch (page 90)

Slip stitch (page 30)

Bar tack (below)

Whipstitch (page 48)

Attaching jump rings
and tassel (page 57)

Weaving in loose ends
(page 36)

A novelty yarn purposely worked
with a small hook to create a
firm fabric gives this little bag a
dressed-up look. The oversized
tassel (we bought one!) adds to
the glamour-girl effect.
Fill your creation with lipstick
and a compact, and you're
ready for an evening out.

Finished Size

Width: 6" (15 cm)

Height: 4" (10 cm)

Materials

Yarn: CYCA classification: 2 Fine, a cord-type
yarn; about 55 yards (53 meters).

Shown here: Noro Daria Multi (55% cotton, 45% rayon; 55 yards [50 meters],
50 grams): #11 ocean/fuchsia/purple, 1
skein.

Hook: Size G/6 (4 mm). Adjust hook size if
necessary to obtain correct gauge.

Notions: 7" (18 cm) zipper in matching color;
sewing needle and thread; pins; yarn needle;
rayon tassel (Conso #11209H–E16 shown);
jump ring, for attaching tassel; needle-nose
pliers, to open jump ring.

Gauge

16 single crochet and 18 rows = 4" (10 cm)
with size G/6 (4 mm) hook.

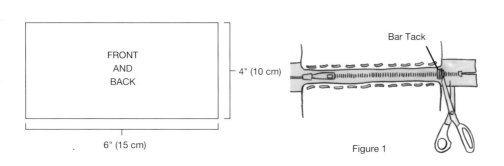

FRONT
AND
BACK

4" (10 cm)

6" (15 cm)

Bar Tack

Figure 1

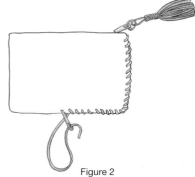

Figure 2

Front/Back (make 2)

Using the hook size needed to obtain the correct gauge, loosely chain 25.

Row 1: Starting with second chain from hook, work 1 single crochet in each chain to end, turn work—24 single crochet.

Row 2: Chain 1, work 1 single crochet in each single crochet, turn work.

Repeat Row 2 until the work measures 4" (10 cm). Fasten off.

Finishing

The yarn used for this project is very dense and cordlike, and the pieces probably won't need blocking. Pin upper edge of each piece to zipper, aligning one end with zipper pull (zipper will be longer than crochet work) and placing piece about ⅛" (3 mm) from zipper teeth (Figure 1). Thread sewing needle with a double strand of sewing thread and using backstitch, sew zipper in place close to edge of crochet. To keep work neat, using sewing needle and single strand of sewing thread, whipstitch outer edges of zipper tape to crochet work. Take care to keep sewing stitches from poking through to the right side of bag. Turn under excess zipper tape at top edge of zipper and stitch in place. Sew a bar tack across lower edge of zipper just beyond edge of bag and cut off excess zipper just below bar tack. Thread yarn needle with extra yarn and, with wrong sides together, whipstitch through both layers of fabric to sew sides and bottom of bag together (Figure 2). Weave in yarn ends through several stitches on wrong side of work. Using needle-nose pliers, open up the jump ring and slide one end under folded edge of the tassel cord and then into zipper tab hole. Carefully close jump ring opening together using pliers.

5

Expanding Knowledge

Now that you have mastered the single crochet projects, you're ready to move on to something a bit more challenging. In this chapter, I am adding a little interest to the mix, so we can explore pattern stitches.

Although the projects in this chapter are still rectangular in shape, the stitches within the rectangles are more complex. As an example, the Neck Gaiter Scarf changes stitches row by row. The headband, both wraps, and the blanket also mix things up. They introduce the idea of creating a pattern through stitch placement (skipping stitches and working more than one stitch in a given place) and replacement (using chains instead of stitches).

But just because the stitches are more complex doesn't mean they are more difficult! There are two keys to crocheting patterns:

⤳ Counting stitches
⤳ Looking at your work

You'll find that counting stitches is more important than ever as you move into these types of projects because the stitch numbers need to remain constant. Also, be sure to make a habit of looking at your work. When you have completed a few pattern repetitions, take a close look at what you've crocheted. Can you see how the pattern falls into place? As you become more and more comfortable with these stitches, it will get easier and easier to see what stitches should go where without constant counting. After a few rows you will be "hooked" and fascinated by the beautiful fabric you are creating.

Neck Gaiter Scarf

Need to know

Gauge (page 35)

Slipknot (page 22)

Chain stitch (page 22)

Turning chain (page 23)

Single crochet (pages 24–25)

Half double crochet
(pages 26–27)

Double crochet (page 28)

Fasten off (page 36)

Changing color (page 32)

Weaving in loose ends
(page 36)

Making corkscrew fringe
(page 61)

This fun piece is an easy way to practice mixing up stitches. It involves single, half double, and double crochet. Vintage buttons and a quirky fringe personalize the look.

Finished Size

Width: 5¼" (13.5 cm)

Length: 23" (58.5 cm), excluding fringe

Materials

Yarn: CYCA classification: 4 Medium, Worsted to Light Bulky Weight; about 50 yards (46 meters) each in 5 colors.

Shown here: Tahki/Stacy Charles Kerry (50% wool, 50% alpaca; 90 yards [83 meters], 50 grams): #5016 Purple (main color), #5005 Orange (A), #5014 Burgundy (B), #5026 Rust (C), #5013 Forest (D); 1 skein each.

Hook: Size J/10 (6 mm). Adjust hook size if necessary to obtain correct gauge.

Notions: 4 buttons, about ⅝" (1.5 cm) in diameter; yarn needle, for working in ends; sewing needle and thread, for sewing buttons.

Gauge

Size J/10 (6 mm) hook used for the following gauges:

14 single crochet and 16 rows = 4" (10 cm)

14 half double crochet and 8 rows = 4" (10 cm)

14 double crochet and 6 rows = 4" (10 cm)

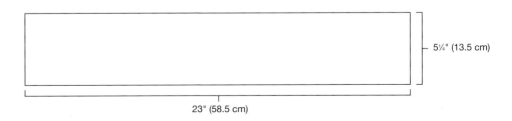

5¼" (13.5 cm)

23" (58.5 cm)

Scarf

Using the hook size needed to obtain correct gauge and main color (MC), loosely chain 19 stitches.

Row 1: With MC, beginning in second chain from hook, work 1 single crochet in each chain to end, turn work—18 single crochet.

Rows 2, 3, and 4: With MC, chain 1, work 1 single crochet in each single crochet to end of row, turn work. Fasten off MC after Row 4 is finished.

Rows 5, 6, 7, and 8: Attach A at the beginning of Row 5, chain 2 (does not count as a stitch), work 1 half double crochet in each stitch to end of row, turn work. Fasten off A after Row 8 is finished.

Rows 9, 10, 11, and 12: Attach MC at beginning of Row 9, repeat Row 2 for each row. Fasten off MC after Row 12 is finished.

Rows 13, 14, and 15: Attach B at the beginning of Row 13, chain 3 (counts as 1 double crochet); beginning with second stitch, work 1 double crochet in each stitch to end of row, turn work. Fasten off B after Row 15 is finished.

Rows 16, 17, 18, and 19: Attach MC at beginning of Row 16, repeat Row 2 for each row. Fasten off MC after Row 19 is finished.

Rows 20, 21, 22, and 23: Attach C at beginning of Row 20, chain 2 (does not count as a stitch), work 1 half double crochet in each stitch to end of row, turn work. Fasten off C after Row 23 is finished.

Rows 24, 25, 26, and 27: Attach MC at beginning of Row 24, repeat Row 2 for each row. Fasten off MC after Row 27 is finished.

Rows 28, 29, and 30: Attach D at beginning of Row 28, chain 3 (counts as one double crochet); beginning with second stitch, work 1 double crochet in each stitch to end of row. Fasten off D after Row 30 is finished.

Rows 31, 32, 33, and 34: Attach MC at beginning of Row 31, repeat Row 2 for each row. Fasten off MC after Row 34 is finished.

Rows 35, 36, 37, and 38: Attach A at the beginning of Row 35, chain 2 (does not count as a stitch), work 1 half double crochet in each stitch to end of row, turn work. Fasten off A after Row 38 is finished.

Rows 39, 40, 41, and 42: Attach MC at beginning of Row 39, repeat Row 2 for each row. Fasten off MC after Row 42 is finished.

Rows 43, 44, and 45: Attach B at the beginning of Row 43, chain 3 (counts as 1 double crochet); beginning with second stitch, work 1 double crochet in each stitch to end of row, turn work. Fasten off B after Row 45 is finished.

Rows 46, 47, 48, and 49: Attach MC at beginning of Row 46, repeat Row 2 for each row. Fasten off MC after Row 49 is finished.

Rows 50, 51, 52, and 53: Attach A at the beginning of Row 50, chain 2 (does not count as a stitch), work 1 half double crochet in each stitch to end of row, turn work. Fasten off A after Row 53 is finished.

Rows 54 and 55: Attach MC at beginning of Row 54, repeat Row 2. Do not fasten off MC.

Row 56 (buttonhole row): With MC chain 1, work 1 single crochet in each of first 2 single crochet, *chain 2, skip next 2 single crochet, work 1 single crochet in each of next 2 single crochet*; repeat from * to * 3 more times across row, turn work (Figures 1 and 2).

Row 57: Chain 1, work 1 single crochet in each of first 2 single crochet, *work 1 single crochet in each of next 2 chains, work 1 single crochet in each of next 2 single crochet*; repeat from * to * 3 more times across row. Fasten off MC.

Finishing

With yarn needle, weave in loose ends. Work corkscrew fringe as follows: Attach MC to upper edge of buttonhole end of scarf, *chain 20, work 1 double crochet in fourth chain from hook, work 2 double crochet in each of next 16 chains, slip-stitch to next stitch along buttonhole edge. Fasten off. Skip 1 stitch, *attach A to next stitch along buttonhole edge and repeat from * to *. Repeat fringe instructions making fringes with B, C, D; skip 2 stitches and repeat from * to * again with MC. Fasten off. With sewing needle and matching thread, sew buttons opposite buttonholes along beginning edge. Lightly block scarf to smooth out stitches if necessary, but do not block corkscrew fringes.

Buttonhole

Figure 1

Figure 2

Making Corkscrew Fringe

Cashmere Headband

Need to know

Gauge (page 35)

Slipknot (page 22)

Chain stitch (page 22)

Turning chain (page 23)

Single crochet (pages 24–25)

Double crochet (page 28)

Whipstitch (page 48)

Slip stitch (page 30)

Weaving in loose ends
(page 36)

More fashion than function, this lacy little accent works up in no time. It's a fun way to try out a pattern stitch without making a major commitment. Cashmere makes it a special gift.

Finished Size

Circumference: 20" (51 cm)

Width: 3" (7.5 cm)

Materials

Yarn: CYCA classification: 3 Light Worsted, cashmere; about 75 yards (69 meters).

Shown here: Plymouth Yarn Royal Cashmere (100% cashmere; 125 yards [114 meters], 50 grams): #8062 red, 1 skein.

Hooks: Size G/6 (4 mm) and size E/4 (3.5 mm). Adjust hook size if necessary to obtain correct gauge.

Notions: Yarn needle, for weaving in loose ends.

Gauge

19 stitches and 7.25 rows = 4" (10 cm) in pattern stitch with size G/6 (4 mm) hook.

Headband

Loosely chain 16.

Row 1: Work 1 double crochet in eighth chain from hook, then work (1 double crochet, chain 1) 3 times into the same chain as the first double crochet (shell made), skip 3 chains, work 1 double crochet into next chain, in the same chain work (1 double crochet, chain 1) 3 times, skip 3 chains, work 1 double crochet in last chain, turn work.

Row 2: Chain 3, *work 1 double crochet into space between second and third double crochet of shell, work (1 double crochet, chain 1) 3 times into same space*; repeat from * to * once more, skip 2 double crochet, skip 2 chains, work 1 double crochet in next chain, turn work.

Row 3: Chain 3, *work 1 double crochet into space between second and third double crochet of shell, work (1 double crochet, chain 1) 3 times into same space*; repeat from * to * in next shell, skip 2 double crochet, work 1 double crochet in top of chain 3.

Repeat Row 3 for pattern until headband measures a total length of about 20" (51 cm) from beginning. Fasten off.

Finishing

With size E/4 (3.5 cm) hook, attach yarn in first chain at right-hand corner of one long edge, work 3 single crochet in first chain 3 or double crochet space, *chain 4, skip stitch between spaces, work 3 single crochet in next chain 3 or double crochet space*; repeat from * to * along edge. Fasten off. Repeat same instructions along the other long edge. Whipstitch short edges together to form the band. Weave in loose ends.

Elegant Chevron Wrap

Need to know

Gauge (page 35)

Making a center-pull ball
(page 97)

Slipknot (page 22)

Chain stitch (page 22)

Turning chain (page 23)

Single crochet (pages 24–25)

Half double crochet
(pages 26–27)

Fasten off (page 36)

Changing colors (page 32)

Stitch markers (page 13)

Slip stitch (page 30)

Light as a cloud and very luxurious, this dramatic wrap features wide border stripes and oversize tassels. The chevron stitch is perennially popular for afghans because it is easy to learn and quick to work up. Here, this familiar stitch takes on a sophisticated air.

Finished Size

Width: 25" (63.5 cm)

Length: 64" (162.5 cm), excluding tassels

Materials

Yarn: CYCA classification: 2 Sport, worked with 2 strands together; about 1,145 yards (1, 047 meters) of main color and 687 yards (628 meters) of each of colors A and B.

Shown here: Rowan's Kidsilk Haze (70% superkid mohair, 30% silk; 229 yards [210 meters], 25 grams): #582 Trance (soft teal [main color]), 5 balls; #597 Jelly (acid green [A]), and #596 Marmalade (orange [B]), 3 balls each.

Hook: Size H/8 (5 mm). Adjust hook size if necessary to obtain correct gauge.

Notions: Yarn needle; cardboard, about 6 × 6" (15 × 15 cm) square, to make tassels.

Gauge

16 stitches and 6 rows = 4" (10 cm) with size H/8 (4 mm) hook in Chevron pattern stitch, with 2 strands of yarn held together.

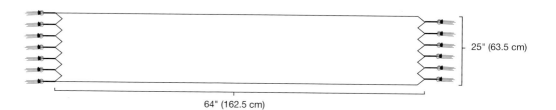

25" (63.5 cm)

64" (162.5 cm)

Pattern Stitch

Chevron Stitch

This stitch is worked over a multiple of 17 + 1 + 3 stitches.

Row 1: Work 2 double crochet in fourth chain from hook, *work 1 double crochet in each of next 7 chains, skip next 2 chains, work 1 double crochet in each of next 7 chains, work 3 double crochet in next chain*; repeat from * to * working only 2 double crochet in last stitch, turn work.

Row 2: Chain 3 (counts as 1 double crochet), work 1 double crochet in first stitch, *work 1 double crochet in each of next 7 double crochet, skip next 2 double crochet, work 1 double crochet in each of next 7 double crochet, work 3 double crochet in next double crochet*; repeat from * to * across row, working only 2 double crochet in last stitch (this stitch will be the top chain of the chain 3 from the beginning of the previous row).

Repeat Row 2 for pattern.

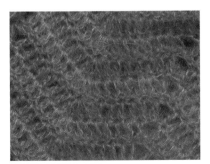

Chevron Stitch

> **Tip: Two strands of yarn are held together as one throughout this project.** Wind the yarn into a center-pull ball (if not already prepared this way) and work using one strand from the center together with the strand from the outer edge of the ball.

Wrap

With B, loosely chain 106. Working in Chevron stitch, begin with Row 1 as listed above and work a total of 10 rows in color B. Fasten off.

Step 1: Attach A and repeat Row 2 for 15 rows. Fasten off.

Step 2: Attach main color (MC) and repeat Row 2 for 55 rows. Fasten off.

Step 3: Attach A and repeat Row 2 for 15 rows. Fasten off.

Step 4: Attach B and repeat Row 2 for 10 rows. Fasten off.

Finishing

Weave in loose ends with a yarn needle. With right side of work facing, attach B at bottom left corner of wrap. Working along short edge of wrap, work 1 single crochet in each of first 9 double crochet, *chain 11, starting in second chain from hook work 1 slip stitch in each chain, work 1 single crochet in each of next 17 double crochet*; repeat from * to * across ending with 1 single crochet in each of last 9 double crochet. Fasten off. With right side of work facing, attach yarn at opposite short edge of wrap, chain 11, starting in second chain from hook work 1 slip stitch in each chain, *work 1 single crochet in each of next 17 double crochet, chain 11, starting in second chain from hook work 1 slip stitch in each chain*; repeat from * to * across. Fasten off.

Tassels
(make 13)

Holding 2 strands of yarn together, wrap yarn around cardboard 15 times to make thirty 12" (30.5 cm) strands. Cut another strand of yarn about 12" (30.5 cm) long and, using a yarn needle, thread this strand under the wrapped strands at the upper edge of the cardboard. Center this strand leaving the same length on each side of the wrapped strands; pull both ends together and tie into a tight knot (Figure 1). Cut across bottom edge of wrapped yarn. Cut another 12" (30.5 cm) strand of yarn and, holding the tassel carefully with all strands laying in the same direction, wrap this strand around the tassel about 1" (2.5 cm) from the top and tie into a knot (Figure 2). Trim ends of this strand to same length as the rest of tassel. Using both ends of upper tie, thread on yarn needle and sew 1 tassel to end of each chain on points of wrap. There will be 6 tassels attached at the short edge where the wrap began and 7 tassels at the other short edge (see schematic for placement). Work ends back into tassel and trim to match. Weave in loose ends with a yarn needle. Block to size.

Making Tassels

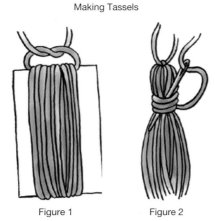

Figure 1   Figure 2

Vibrant V-Stitch Wrap

Need to know

Gauge (page 35)

Slipknot (page 22)

Chain stitch (page 22)

Turning chain (page 23)

Single crochet (pages 24–25)

Double crochet (page 28)

Slip stitch (page 30)

Weaving in loose ends
(page 36)

> The important thing to remember is to keep the stitch count constant: Wherever a stitch is skipped, it needs to be replaced either by a chain or by more than one stitch in adjacent stitch(es).

Now that you've mastered the basic stitches, try grouping and separating them in a repeating pattern to create beautiful, lacy pattern stitches. By using a longer stitch and a relatively large hook, the fabric created here will have a beautiful drape that's just right for this wrap.

Finished Size

Width: 22" (56 cm)

Length: 69" (175 cm)

Materials

Yarn: CYCA classification: 3 DK or Light Worsted; about 1,500 yards (1,372 meters).

Shown here: Dale of Norway Svale (50% cotton, 40% viscose, 10% silk; 114 yards [104 meters], 50 grams): # 4227 dark red, 14 balls.

Hook: Size H/8 (5 mm). Adjust hook size if necessary to obtain correct gauge.

Notions: Yarn needle, for weaving in loose ends.

Gauge

31 stitches and 14 rows = 8" (20.5 cm) in pattern stitch with size H/8 (5 mm) hook.

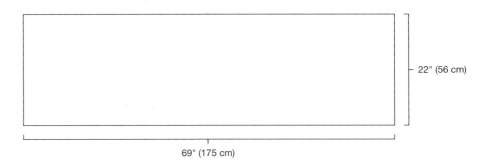

22" (56 cm)

69" (175 cm)

Wrap

Using the appropriate hook size to obtain correct gauge, loosely chain 87 stitches.

Row 1: Starting in second chain from hook work 1 single crochet in each chain, turn work— 86 single crochet.

Row 2: Chain 1, work 1 single crochet in each single crochet, turn work.

Rows 3 and 4: Repeat Row 2.

Row 5 (begin pattern): Chain 3 (counts as 1 double crochet), skip first 2 single crochet, *work 2 double crochet in each of next 2 single crochet, skip next 2 single crochet*; repeat from * to * to last 2 single crochet, skip next single crochet, work 1 double crochet in last single crochet, turn work.

Row 6: Chain 3 (counts as 1 double crochet), skip first 2 double crochet, *work 2 double crochet in each of next 2 double crochet, skip next 2 double crochet*; repeat from * to * across to last 2 stitches, skip 1 double crochet, work 1 double crochet in top chain of turning chain from previous row (last stitch).

Repeat Row 6 until piece measures 68" (173 cm) from beginning chain edge. Work 4 rows in single crochet, fasten off.

Finishing

Weave in loose ends. Steam lightly as needed.

Stimulating Stripes Baby Blanket

Need to know

Gauge (page 35)

Slipknot (page 22)

Chain stitch (page 22)

Turning chain (page 23)

Single crochet (pages 24–25)

Double crochet (page 28)

Slip stitch (page 30)

Making and attaching tassel
  (page 67)

Weaving in loose ends
  (page 36)

Vibrant colors give traditional stitches an up-to-the-minute look for that forward-thinking baby (or parent). Although the border is a little more elaborate, the blanket itself is a striped variation of close scallops, a simple shell-pattern stitch. The stitches are closely spaced to prevent tiny fingers from getting caught. The border is worked separately on each side and then tied together with tassel-edged cords.

Finished Size

Without border: 30 × 30" (76 x 76 cm)

With border: 36 × 36" (91.5 x 91.5 cm)

Materials

Yarn: CYCA classification: 3 DK or Light Worsted; about 400 yards (366 meters) each of 3 colors A, B, C; and about 200 yards (183 meters) color D.

Shown here: Brown Sheep Cotton Fleece (80% pima cotton, 20% merino wool; 215 yards [197 meters], 100 grams): CW345 Gold Dust (A), CW220 Provincial Rose (B), and CW840 Lime Light (C), 2 skeins each; CW765 Blue Paradise (D), 1 skein.

Hook: Size H/8 (5 mm). Adjust hook size if necessary to obtain correct gauge.

Notions: Yarn needle, for weaving in ends; safety pins, for marking border; 2" (5 cm) square of cardboard, for measuring tassels.

Gauge

25 stitches = 8" (20.5 cm) and 8 rows = 4" (10 cm) with size H/8 (5 mm) hook in close scallops pattern stitch.

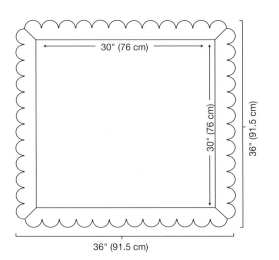

Pattern Stitch
Close Scallops

Beginning chain requires multiple of 6 stitches + 1. Basic pattern (Row 2) is worked over a multiple of 5 stitches + 4.

Row 1 (preparation row): Work 2 double crochet into fourth chain from hook, skip next 2 chains, work 1 single crochet in next chain, *skip 2 chains, work 4 double crochet in next chain, skip 2 chains, work 1 single crochet in next chain*; repeat from * to * across, turn work.

Row 2: Chain 3 (counts as 1 double crochet), work 2 double crochet in first single crochet, skip 2 double crochet, *work 1 single crochet between second and third double crochet of next shell group, skip 2 double crochet, work 4 double crochet in next single crochet, skip 2 double crochet*; repeat from * to * across row, ending with 1 single crochet in space between last double crochet and beginning chain 3 of previous row, turn work.

Repeat Row 2 for pattern.

Blanket

With A, loosely chain 115. Work close scallops pattern as follows:

Row 1 (preparation row): With A, work 2 double crochet into fourth chain from hook, skip next 2 chains, work 1 single crochet in next chain, *skip 2 chains, work 4 double crochet in next chain, skip 2 chains, work 1 single crochet in next chain*; repeat from * to * across row, turn work—94 stitches, including beginning chain 3.

Row 2: Chain 3 (counts as 1 double crochet), work 2 double crochet in first single crochet, skip 2 double crochet, *work 1 single crochet between second and third double crochet of next shell group, skip 2 double crochet, work 4 double crochet in next single crochet, skip 2 double crochet*; repeat from * to * across row, ending with 1 single crochet in space between last double crochet and chain 3 of previous row, turn work—94 stitches. Fasten off.

Rows 3 and 4: Attach B, repeat Row 2. Fasten off.
Rows 5 and 6: Attach C, repeat Row 2. Fasten off.

Continue repeating Row 2 throughout blanket and working 2 rows each in the A, B, and C color sequence until blanket measures a total length of 30" (76 cm) or 60 rows total (30 stripes). Fasten off. Weave in loose ends.

Border

The four-row border pattern is worked along each blanket edge separately. After the border is finished, long crochet chains are used to decoratively lace the corner edges together.

Beginning with the edge at last close scallops pattern row, attach D and work border as follows.

Row 1: Chain 3 (counts as 1 double crochet), work 1 double crochet in the same space, work 1 double crochet in each stitch across row to last stitch, work 2 double crochet in last stitch, turn work—96 stitches.

Row 2: Chain 1, work 1 single crochet in each of first 3 double crochet, *chain 2, skip 1 double crochet, in next double crochet work (2 double crochet, chain 2) twice, skip 1 double crochet, work 1 single crochet in each of next 5 double crochet*; repeat from * to * 10 more times, then work last repeat as chain 2, skip 1 double crochet, in next double crochet work (2 double crochet, chain 2) twice, skip 1 double crochet, work 1 single crochet in each of last 3 stitches (includes chain 3 of previous row), turn work.

Row 3: Chain 1, work 1 single crochet in each of first 2 single crochet, *chain 3, skip next chain-2 space, in next chain-2 space work (3 double crochet, chain 2, 3 double crochet), chain 3, skip 1 single crochet, work 1 single crochet in each of next 3 single crochet*; repeat from * to * 10 more times, then work final repeat as chain 3, skip next chain-2 space, in next chain-2 space work (3 double crochet, chain 2, 3 double crochet), chain 3, skip 1 single crochet, work 1 single crochet in each of next 2 single crochet, turn work.

Row 4: Chain 1, work 1 single crochet in first single crochet, *chain 4, skip next chain-3 space, in next chain-2 space work (4 double crochet, chain 2, 4 double crochet), chain 4, skip 1 single crochet, work 1 single crochet in next single crochet*; repeat from * to * to end of row. Fasten off.

Opposite edge

Turn blanket to opposite edge (chain edge).

Attach D to one end of chain edge and begin Row 1 by working chain 3 (counts as 1 double crochet), then work 95 double crochet into the spaces above the chain edge, instead of into the individual chains. Make sure the stitches are evenly spaced across the entire row, turn work—96 double crochet, including the beginning chain 3. Continue border pattern along this edge by working Rows 2–4 same as previous edge.

Side edges

For blanket side edges attach D and begin Row 1 with chain 3 (counts as 1 double crochet), work a total of 96 double crochet evenly spaced along each side edge.

To evenly space stitches along the side edges, either mark into quarters with safety pins and pick up 25 percent of stitches between pins; or work 2 double crochet in same space as chain 3, 2 double crochet in each of first 3 spaces, then alternate 1 double crochet in next space, 2 double crochet in following space to last 3 spaces, work 2 double crochet in last spaces to add up to 96 stitches. Continue to work Border Pattern through Row 4, fasten off.

Finishing

Weave in loose ends. Using 2" (5 cm) piece of cardboard as a guide, make 8 tassels with A by winding yarn around cardboard 22 times (Figures 1 and 2, page 67). With A, make 4 chains of 80 stitches each. Lace chains through spaces in each corner of border (like a shoelace), beginning at first row of border and ending at outside edge.

When all four corners are laced, attach one tassel to each end of crochet chains and tie each chain into a bow.

6

Taking Shape

In this chapter, the emphasis is on shaping. It is time to move beyond the rectangle!

I've kept the stitches simple, so you can focus on the following three techniques, which are key to creating crocheted shapes:

- Increasing stitches
- Decreasing stitches
- Working partial rows

Armed with these skills, you'll be able to create any shape you can imagine.

In addition to shaping, these projects also showcase versatility. The more you crochet, the more possibilities you can see. The two evening bags featured here, a dressy version and a casual version, are virtually the same pattern with a change in gauge and trim. The Button-Front Top offers several variations, and the Funky Stuffed Toys have plenty of room for self-expression. There is no limit to the possible color combinations. Even changing the yarn texture will give you a whole new angle on these beautiful, shapely projects.

Casual Evening Bag

Need to know

Gauge (page 35)

Slipknot (page 22)

Chain stitch (page 22)

Turning chain (page 23)

Single crochet (pages 24–25)

Working into the front loops
(page 24)

Decreases (page 31)

Stitch markers (page 13)

Fasten off (page 36)

Weaving in loose ends
(page 36)

Whipstitch (page 48)

Making fringe (page 39)

Blocking (page 36)

Abbreviations

ch   chain stitch

sc   single crochet

This one simple bag offers two distinct personalities depending on the yarn you choose. Either way, this bag is a handy size for those evening essentials—keys, cash, cosmetics—and the long strap lets you keep it close without having to hang on. A ribbonlike yarn makes a casual version; a metallic yarn creates a dressy version.

Finished Size

Width: 5½" (14 cm)

Length: 7" (18 cm)

Strap length after attached to sides of bag: 50"
(127 cm)

Materials

Yarn: CYCA classification: 4 Worsted, ribbon yarn; about 225 yards (206 meters).

Shown here: Berroco Suede (100 % nylon; 120 yards [110 meters], 50 grams): #3717, 2 balls.

Hook: Size F/5 (3.75 mm). Adjust hook size if necessary to obtain correct gauge.

Notions: Safety pins, to designate right side of work and hold pieces together for sewing; 1 button, ⅞" (2.2 cm) in diameter; yarn needle, for sewing pieces together and weaving in loose ends; 6" (15 cm) square piece of heavy cardboard, to measure fringe.

Gauge

19 stitches and 19 rows = 4" (10 cm) in single crochet with size F/5 (3.75 mm) hook.

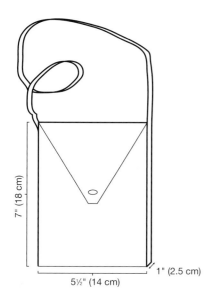

7" (18 cm)

1" (2.5 cm)

5½" (14 cm)

Strap Length above bag sides

Casual Bag: 50" (127 cm)

Dressy Bag: 40" (101.5 cm)

Main Piece (Front, Back, Flap)

Beginning at top front edge, loosely ch 27.

Row 1: Beginning in second ch from hook, work 1 sc in each ch to end of row, turn work—26 sc.

Note: The work will look the same on both sides. Designate one side as the right side of the work and mark it with a safety pin.

Row 2: Ch 1, work 1 sc in each sc, turn work—26 sc.

Repeat Row 2 until piece measures 7" (18 cm), ending with a completed right-side row.

Next row (fold line): With wrong side of work facing, ch1, and continuing in sc, work into front loop of stitch only (see page 24), across row, turn work.

Next 3 rows: Work in sc same as Row 2, and inserting the hook through both loops of each sc.

Next row (wrong side): Repeat fold line row, working into front loop only.

Continue in sc, repeating Row 2 as before until back measures same length as Front, ending with a completed right-side row.

Next Row (wrong side): Repeat fold line row.

Shape flap

Row 1: With right side of work facing, work 1 sc in first sc, work decrease in next 2 stitches by working them together (insert hook in next stitch, pull up a loop, insert hook in next stitch pull up a loop, wrap yarn around hook and pull through all 3 loops on hook), work in sc as established to last 3 stitches, decrease in next 2 stitches, work 1 sc in last stitch, turn work—24 sc.

Row 2: Ch 1, work 1 sc in each sc, turn work.

Repeat Rows 1 and 2 until 8 stitches remain, ending with a right-side row completed.

Buttonhole Row (wrong side of work): Ch 1, work 1 sc in each of first 2 sc, ch 4, skip next 4 sc, work 1 sc in each of last 2 sc, turn work.

Next row: Ch 1, work 1 sc, make decrease by working together second sc and first ch of buttonhole, work 1 sc in each of next 2 ch, make second decrease by working together fourth ch of buttonhole and next sc, work 1 sc in last single crochet, turn work—6 sc.

Continue work as established repeating Rows 1 and 2 until 4 stitches remain. Fasten off.

Sides and Strap
Loosely ch 5 stitches.

Row 1: Ch 1, beginning in second ch from hook, work 1 sc in each ch to end of row, turn work—4 sc.
Row 2: Ch 1, work 1 sc in each sc, turn work.

Repeat Row 2 until piece measures 64" (162.5 cm). Fasten off.

Finishing
Weave in loose ends. Using fold lines as a guide, fold main piece to make the Front, Back, and Flap sections. With safety pins, pin one end of strap along the side edges of both Front and Back, from bottom edge to top; repeat with other strap end along second side edges of Front and Back. (After attaching the strap, 7" [18 cm] at each strap end form the purse sides; the remaining 50" [127 cm] length becomes the strap.) With wrong sides together, sew strap neatly in place using whipstitch. Mark

button placement to match buttonhole and sew button in place. Using cardboard as a guide, cut 30 pieces of fringe, each 12" (30.5 cm) long (Figure 1, page 39). Using crochet hook, pull fringe through and knot along center of bottom edge and on flap end (Figure 2, page 39). Steam lightly as needed.

Dressy Evening Bag

Tip: The lesson here is on simple shaping. The decreases are worked inside the edge rather than on the edge stitch. This keeps the edge smooth and eliminates the need for a border.

Finished Size

Width: 5½" (14 cm)
Length: 7" (18 cm)
Strap length after attached to sides of bag: 40" (101.5 cm)

Materials

Yarn: CYCA classification: 2 Fine, sportweight metallic ribbon; about 300 yards (274 meters).

Shown here: Plymouth 24K (82% nylon, 18% lamé; 187 yards [171 meters], 50 grams): #61, 2 balls.

Hook: Size E/4 (3.5 mm). Adjust hook size if necessary to obtain correct gauge.

Notions: 1 button, about ¾" (2 cm) in diameter; safety pins, to mark right side of work and hold pieces together for sewing; yarn needle, for sewing pieces together and weaving in loose ends.

Gauge

26 stitches and 24 rows = 4" (10 cm) with size E/4 (3.5 mm) hook in single crochet.

Main Piece (Front, Back, Flap)
Loosely ch 37.

Row 1: Beginning in second ch from hook, work 1 sc in each ch to end of row, turn work—36 sc.

Row 2: Ch 1, work 1 sc in each sc. Work as for Casual Evening Bag, working buttonhole row when 12 stitches remain.

Buttonhole Row (wrong side of work): Ch 1, work 1 sc in each of first 4 sc, ch 4, skip next 4 sc, work 1 sc in each of last 4 sc, turn work.

Next row (right side of work): Ch 1, work 1 sc in first sc, work decrease as established over next 2 stitches, work 1 sc in next sc, work 1 sc in each of next 4 ch, work 1 sc in next sc, work decrease as established over next 2 sc, work 1 sc in last sc, turn work—10 sc.

Continue as for Casual Evening Bag until 6 stitches remain. Fasten off.

Sides and Strap

Ch 6

Row 1: Beginning in second ch from hook, work 1 sc in each ch to end of row, turn work—5 sc.
Row 2: Ch 1, work 1 sc in each sc, turn work. Repeat Row 2 until piece measures 54" (137 cm). Fasten off.

Finishing

Finish as for Casual Evening Bag, omitting fringe. Remaining strap length will be 40" (101.5 cm) after attaching strap to both side edges of bag.

Funky Stuffed Toys

Need to know

Gauge (page 35)

Slipknot (page 22)

Chain stitch (page 22)

Single crochet (pages 24–25)

Whipstitch (page 48)

Weaving in loose ends
(page 36)

Single crochet decrease
(page 31)

Fasten off (page 36)

Changing colors (page 32)

Abbreviations

ch chain stitch

sc single crochet

Bright colors and simple details define this cat and dog. They are a great exercise in striping, with a little shaping thrown in. Stuff them tightly or slightly for different looks. Whipstitched seams add another touch of color and emphasize the handmade look. With the exception of the ears and tails, both animals are constructed the same, just in different colors.

Finished Size

About 13¼" (33.5 cm) long and 4" (10 cm) wide, excluding arms and ears.

Materials

Yarn: CYCA classification: 3 Light Worsted-weight cotton, about 200 yards (183 meters) total per animal.

Shown here: Tahki Cotton Classic (100% mercerized cotton; 108 yards [100 meters], 50 grams): #3412 orange (A), #3528 yellow (B), #3744 dark green (C), #3764 bright green (D), #3783 turquoise (E), #3856 navy (F), and #3947 red violet (G). For Cat, use 1 skein each of A, C, D, E, G; for Dog, use 1 skein each of A, B, C, D, E, F, G. (Note: The total number of skeins listed above will make more than 2 animals.)

Hook: Size G/6 (4 mm). Adjust hook size if necessary to obtain the correct gauge.

Notions: Yarn needle, for sewing and weaving in ends; two⅜" (1 cm) diameter buttons per animal, for eyes; stuffing (either cotton batting or polyester fiberfill).

Gauge

20 stitches and 24 rows = 4" (10 cm) in sc with size G/6 (4 mm) hook.

Cat

With color E, ch 21.

Row 1: Beginning in second ch from hook, work 1 sc in each ch, turn work—20 sc.

Row 2: Ch 1, work 1 sc in each sc across row, turn work.

Rows 3 and 4: Repeat Row 2. Fasten off E.

Rows 5–8: Using color G, repeat Row 2. Fasten off G.

Repeating Row 2, continue to alternate 4 rows with E, followed by 4 rows with G for a total of 28 rows. Fasten off.

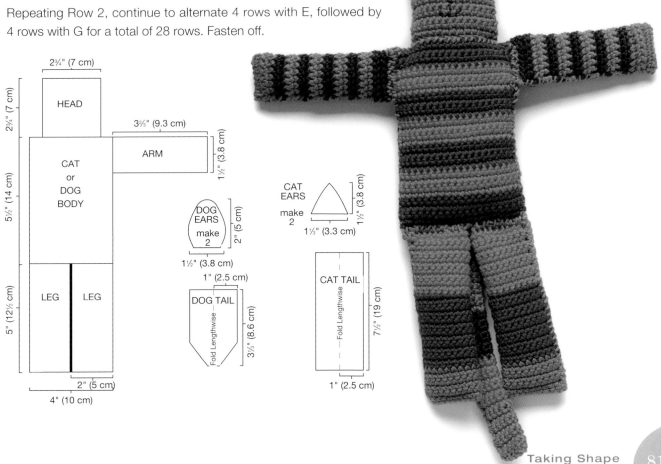

2¾" (7 cm)

2¾" (7 cm)

HEAD

3⅔" (9.3 cm)

ARM

1½" (3.8 cm)

5½" (14 cm)

CAT or DOG BODY

5" (12½ cm)

LEG   LEG

2" (5 cm)

4" (10 cm)

DOG EARS make 2

2" (5 cm)

1½" (3.8 cm)

1" (2.5 cm)

DOG TAIL

Fold Lengthwise

3⅓" (8.6 cm)

CAT EARS make 2

1½" (3.8 cm)

1⅓" (3.3 cm)

CAT TAIL

Fold Lengthwise

7½" (19 cm)

1" (2.5 cm)

Front

With G, ch 21. Work as for Back, alternating 4 rows in G, followed by 4 rows in A for a total of 28 rows. Fasten off.

Head (make 2 pieces)

With D, ch 15.

Row 1: Beginning in second ch from hook, work 1 sc in each ch, turn work—14 sc.
Row 2: Ch 1, work 1 sc in each sc across row, turn work.

Repeat Row 2 until head measures a total length of about 2¾" (7 cm) or 16 rows. Fasten off.

Arms (make 2, worked from shoulder down)

With color C, ch 16.

Row 1: Beginning in second chain from hook, work 1 sc in each ch, turn work—15 sc.
Row 2: Ch 1, work 1 sc in each sc across row, turn work.
Note: Don't fasten off C. Allow the unused color to hang at the side edge and pull up into place when ready to use again. Don't pull yarn up too tightly, or work will pucker along side edge.

Rows 3 and 4: Using color E, repeat Row 2. Don't fasten off E.

Drop E and pick up C where it hangs along side edge. Continue to repeat Row 2, alternating 2 rows with C followed by 2 rows with E for a total of 18 rows. Fasten off

C and E. Attach D and work 4 rows sc (repeating Row 2). Fasten off.

Legs (make 2, worked from thigh down)

With color A, ch 21.

Row 1: Beginning in second ch from hook, work 1 sc in each ch, turn work—20 sc.
Row 2: Ch 1, work 1 sc in each sc across row, turn work.

Repeat Row 2 until work measures 2" (5 cm). Fasten off A. Attach G and continue repeating Row 2 for an additional 2" (5 cm). Fasten off G. Attach D and continue repeating Row 2 for 1" (2.5 cm). Fasten off D.

Tail: (worked from tip to top)

With color E, ch 11.

Row 1: Beginning in second ch from hook, work 1 sc in each ch, turn work—10 sc.
Row 2: Ch 1, work 1 sc in each sc across row, turn work.

Repeat Row 2 until tail measures 1½" (3.8 cm). Fasten off E. *Join A, repeat Row 2 for 1½" (3.8 cm). Fasten off*. Repeat from * to * in colors C, D, and G. Finished tail measures 7½" (19 cm), and each color section is 1½" (3.8 cm) long.

Ears (make 2)

With color A, ch 8.

Row 1: Beginning in second ch from hook, work 1 sc in each ch, turn work—7 sc.

Row 2: Ch 1, work 1 sc in each sc across row, turn work.

Row 3: Ch 1, decrease 1 stitch by pulling up a loop in first sc, pull up a loop in second sc, wrap yarn around hook, pull through all loops on hook (see page 31), work 1 sc in each of remaining sc, turn work—6 sc. Repeat Row 3 five more times (1 stitch remains). Fasten off.

Finishing

Weave in loose ends. To create face, with color G, sew buttons for eyes on 1 head piece and embroider nose/mouth as shown in diagram (page 84). If you prefer, omit buttons for eyes and embroider 2 triangles (not shown here) in same place as buttons. Use whipstitch on right sides of work (seaming is visible) to sew all pieces together. With E, join both head pieces together around side and upper edges, leaving the bottom open. With the face side toward you, place the ears in front of the head seam and attach to top of head piece. Whipstitch around edges of ears. Mark center of each head piece and center of body front and back. Center head over body and join front and back together at shoulders. Sew body side seams and stuff head and body as desired. Stitch along bottom edges of body to close. Fold tail lengthwise with wrong sides together and stitch along the long edge and across chain edge. Sew open end of tail to lower edge of center back. Fold arms in half lengthwise with wrong sides together and stitch along side and lower edges. Stuff arms as desired. Sew open edges of arm to close. Fold leg pieces in half lengthwise with wrong sides together and sew along side and lower edges. Stuff legs as for arms. Sew open edges of leg to close. Attach arms and legs in place to body.

Dog

Back

Work same as for Cat, beginning with C, and alternating 4 rows each in C and G for a total of 28 rows.

Front

Work same as for Cat, beginning with G and alternating 4 rows each in G, then B, for a total of 28 rows.

Head (make 2 pieces)

Work same as for Cat, using A.

Arms (make 2, worked from shoulder down)

Work same as for Cat, beginning with D and alternating 2 rows each in D, then E, for a total of 18 rows. Attach A and work 4 rows.

Legs (make 2, worked from thigh down)

Work same as for Cat in 2" (5 cm) segments beginning with F, then E. With A, work final 1" (2.5 cm).

Tail (worked from top down to tip)

With E, ch 11.

Row 1: Beginning in second ch from hook, work sc in each ch, turn work—10 sc.

Row 2: Ch 1, work 1 sc in each sc across row, turn work. Fasten off E.

Repeat Row 2 working 2 rows each in D, C, F, G, A, B; don't fasten off B. Continue working in B and decrease 1 stitch at beginning of next 6 rows by pulling up a loop in first sc, pull up a loop in second sc, wrap yarn around hook, pull through all loops on hook (see page 31)—4 sc remain. Fasten off.

Ears: With color G, ch 7.

Row 1: Beginning in second ch from hook, work sc in each ch, turn work—6 sc.

Row 2: Ch 1, work 1 sc in each sc across row, turn work.

Row 3: Ch 1, work 2 sc in first sc, work 1 sc in each of next 4 sc, work 2 sc in last sc, turn work—8 sc. Repeating Row 2, work 3 rows in sc over 8 stitches.

Rows 7–12: Ch 1, decrease 1 stitch (work decreases using the same method as in tail), work 1 sc in each sc across row, turn work (2 sc remain after Row 12 is finished). Fasten off.

Finishing

Follow finishing instructions for Cat, except use B for face embroidery and whipstitch seaming. Place ears on top of head, aligning edge of ear with side of head; there will be a small space centered between the ears.

□ 1 Single Crochet

I Back Stitch

✕ Cross Stitch

☺ Button for Eye

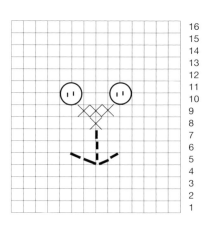

Button-Front Top

Need to know

Gauge (page 35)

Slipknot (page 22)

Chain stitch (page 22)

Turning chain (page 23)

Half double crochet
 (pages 26–27)

Treble crochet (page 29)

Work even (page 30)

Slip stitch (page 30)

Fasten off (page 36)

Abbreviations

ch   chain stitch

hdc   half double crochet

sl st   slip stitch

tr   treble crochet

This little top, made with simple stitches, is a good exercise in making the curved shapes that create armholes and necklines. The design allows you to make several easy variations. Follow the instructions as they are written to create a button-up tank with a ruffled bottom. Or skip the ruffled bottom for a sleeker look. Don't have the time to deal with buttons? Go even simpler yet by joining together two backs for a quick yet elegant tank.

Finished Size

To fit size XS (S, M, L, XL), finished bust measures 30 (34, 38, 42, 46)" (76 [86.5, 96.5, 106.5, 117] cm)

Size shown: Small, 34" (86.5 cm)

Note: Instructions are given for smallest size with larger sizes in parentheses. Where there is only one instruction or number, it applies to all sizes.

Materials

Yarn: CYCA classification: 3 Light Worsted Weight, about 589 (675, 746, 907, 987) yards (538.5 [617, 682, 829, 902] meters).

Shown here: Rowan Summer Tweed (70% silk, 30% cotton; 118 yards [108 meters], 50 grams): #537 summer berry, 5 (6, 7, 8, 9) skeins.

Hook: Size H/8 (5 mm). Adjust hook size if necessary to obtain correct gauge.

Notions: 5 vintage buttons, about 1" (2.5 cm) in diameter; safety pins, for stitch markers; yarn needle, for sewing front and back together; sewing needle and thread, for sewing buttons.

Gauge

12 hdc = 3½" (9 cm) and 10 rows = 4" (10 cm) with size H/8 (5 mm) hook.

Tip: When instructions direct you to work a certain number of stitches evenly along an edge, use safety pins to divide the whole area into four sections and then work 25 percent of the required number of stitches in each section. This method will keep your work more even and also allow you to see in the first section just how close—or how far apart—to place stitches, thereby setting the pace for the entire length.

Back

Loosely ch 54 (60, 68, 74, 80).

Row 1: Beginning in third ch from hook, work 1 hdc in each ch—52 (58, 66, 72, 78) stitches.

Row 2: Ch 2 (does not count as stitch), beginning in first hdc, work 1 hdc in each hdc to end of row, turn work—52 (58, 66, 72, 78) hdc.

Mark right side of work with a safety pin. Repeat Row 2 until back measures a total length of 12½ (13, 13, 14, 14)" (31.5 [33, 33, 35.5, 35.5] cm) from beginning, ending with a completed wrong-side row.

Shape armhole

Row 1 (right side): Sl st across first 4 stitches, ch 2 (does not count as stitch), work 1 hdc in each hdc as established until 4 hdc remain, turn work, leaving remaining stitches unworked—44 (50, 58, 64, 70) hdc.

Row 2 (wrong side): Sl st across first 2 (2, 3, 3, 3) stitches, ch 2 (does not count as stitch), work 1 hdc in each hdc as established until 2 (2, 3, 3, 3) hdc remain, turn work, leaving remaining stitches unworked—40 (46, 52, 58, 64) hdc.

Row 3: Sl st across 1 (1, 2, 2, 2) stitch(es), ch 2 (does not count as stitch), work 1 hdc in each hdc as established until 1 (1, 2, 2, 2) hdc remain, turn work, leaving remaining stitches unworked—38 (44, 48, 54, 60) hdc.

Row 4: Sl st across 0 (1, 1, 2, 2) stitch(es), ch 2 (does not count as stitch), work 1 hdc in each hdc as established until 0 (1, 1, 2, 2) hdc remain, turn work, leaving remaining stitches unworked—38 (42, 46, 50, 56) hdc.

Row 5: Sl st across 0 (1, 1, 1, 1) stitch, ch 2 (does not count as stitch), work 1 hdc in each hdc as established until 0 (1, 1, 1, 1) hdc remains, turn work, leaving remaining stitch unworked—38 (40, 44, 48, 54) hdc.

Sizes XS, S, and M only, work as follows:

Row 6: Ch 2 (does not count as stitch), work 1 hdc in each 38 (40, 44) hdc.

Repeat Row 6 until armhole measures about 3 (3½, 3½)" [7.5 (9, 9) cm], ending with a wrong-side row completed, then follow instructions for back right neck and right shoulder strap (all sizes).

Sizes L and XL only, work as follows:

Row 6: Sl st across 1 stitch, ch 2 (does not count as stitch), work 1 hdc in each hdc as established until 1 hdc remains, turn work, leaving remaining stitch unworked—(46, 52) hdc.

Repeat Row 6 one more time for size L and 2 more times for size XL—(44, 48) hdc.

Continue to work sizes L and XL as follows:

Ch 2 (does not count as stitch), work 1 hdc in (44, 48) hdc to end of row.

Repeat this row until armhole measures about 4½" (11.5 cm) ending with a wrong-side row completed, then follow instructions for Shape Back right neck and right shoulder strap (all sizes).

Tip: Both sides of the work will look similar. To designate a right side and a wrong side, place a safety pin on the side that should face the public, not your body, when the piece is finished.

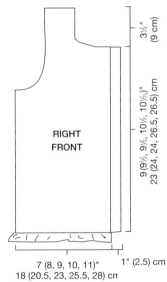

2¼ (2¼, 3, 3, 3½)"
5.5 (5.5, 7.5, 7.5, 9) cm

6½ (7, 7, 7, 7)"
16.5 (18, 18, 18, 18) cm

6½ (7, 7, 8, 8)"
16.5 (18, 18, 20.5, 20.5) cm

BACK

12½ (13, 13, 14, 14)"
31.5 (33, 33, 35.5, 35.5) cm

1" (2.5) cm

15 (17, 19, 21, 23)"
38 (43, 48.5, 53.5, 58.5)cm

3½ "
(9 cm)

RIGHT FRONT

9 (9½, 9½, 10½, 10½)"
23 (24, 24, 26.5, 26.5) cm

7 (8, 9, 10, 11)"
18 (20.5, 23, 25.5, 28) cm

1" (2.5) cm

Shape back right neck and right shoulder strap (all sizes)

Row 1 (right side): At armhole edge, ch 2 (does not count as stitch), beginning in first hdc, work 1 hdc in each of next 14 (14, 16, 16, 18) hdc, turn work, leaving remaining 24 (26, 28, 28, 30) stitches unworked.

Row 2 (wrong side): At neck edge, sl st across first 3 stitches, ch 2 (does not count as stitch), work 1 hdc in each of 11 (11, 13, 13, 15) hdc to end of row, turn work.

Row 3: Ch 2 (does not count as stitch), beginning in first hdc, work 1 hdc in each of 9 (9, 11, 11, 13) hdc, turn work, leaving remaining stitches unworked.

Row 4: Sl st across 1 stitch, ch 2 (does not count as hdc), work 1 hdc in each of remaining 8 (8, 10, 10, 12) hdc, turn work.

Row 5: Ch 2 (does not count as stitch), beginning in first hdc, work 1 hdc in each of next 8 (8, 10, 10, 12) hdc, turn work.

Repeat Row 5 until armhole depth measures 6½ (7, 7, 8, 8)" (16.5 [18, 18, 20.5, 20.5] cm). Fasten off. Cut yarn leaving 4" (10 cm) tail to weave in later.

Shape back left neck and left shoulder strap

Row 1 (right side): Beginning on the first neckline row same as right neck, skip the center 10 (12, 12, 12, 12) stitches, rejoin yarn in next hdc, ch 2 (does not count as stitch), work 1 hdc in same stitch as yarn was joined and in each hdc to end of row—14 (14, 16, 16, 18) hdc.

Row 2 (wrong side): At armhole edge, ch 2 (does not count as stitch), beginning in first stitch, work 1 hdc in each of 11 (11, 13, 13, 15) hdc, turn work, leaving remaining stitches unworked.

Row 3: Beginning at neck edge, sl st across first 2 stitches, ch 2 (does not count as stitch), work 1 hdc in each of 9 (9, 11, 11, 13) hdc, turn work.

Row 4: Ch 2, beginning in first hdc, work 1 hdc in each of 8 (8, 10, 10, 12) hdc, turn work, leaving remaining stitch unworked.

Repeat Row 4 working across 8 (8, 10, 10, 12) hdc until armhole depth measures 6½ (7, 7, 8, 8)" (16.5 [18, 18, 20.5, 20.5] cm), or same length as opposite side. Fasten off. Cut yarn leaving 4" (10 cm) tail to weave in later.

Left Front (as worn)
Loosely ch 26 (30, 34, 36, 40).

Row 1: Beginning with third ch from hook, work 1 hdc in each ch for a total of 24 (28, 32, 34, 38) hdc, turn work.

Row 2: Ch 2 (does not count as stitch), beginning in first hdc work 1 hdc in each hdc to end of row, turn work—24 (28, 32, 34, 38) hdc.

Mark the right side of work with a safety pin. Repeat Row 2 until front measures same as back to beginning of armhole shaping, ending with a completed wrong-side row.

Shape armhole

Row 1 (right side): Beginning at armhole edge, sl st across first 4 stitches, ch 2 (does not count as stitch), work 1 hdc in each of 20 (24, 28, 30, 34) hdc to end of row, turn work.

Row 2 (wrong side): At center front edge, ch 2 (does not count as stitch), beginning in first stitch work 1 hdc in each of 18 (22, 25, 27, 31) hdc, turn work, leaving remaining stitches unworked.

Row 3: Sl st across 1 (1, 2, 2, 2) stitch(es), ch 2 (does not count as stitch), work 1 hdc in each of 17 (21, 23, 25, 29) hdc to end of row, turn work.

Row 4: Ch 2, beginning in first stitch work 1 hdc in each of 17 (20, 22, 23, 27) hdc, turn work, leaving remaining 0 (1, 1, 2, 2) stitch(es) unworked.

Row 5: Sl st across 0 (1, 1, 1, 1) stitch(es), ch 2, work 1 hdc in each of 17 (19, 21, 22, 26) hdc, turn work.

Row 6: Ch 2, beginning in first stitch work 1 hdc in each of 17 (19, 20, 21, 25) hdc, turn work, leaving remaining 0 (0, 1, 1, 1) stitch(es) unworked.

Sizes XS, S, and M only: Repeat Row 6 working 17 (19, 20) hdc until armhole measures 3 (3½, 3½)" [7.5 (9, 9) cm], ending with a completed wrong-side row, then continue front following instructions under "Shape Neck (all sizes)."

Sizes L and XL only, continue as follows:

Row 7: Sl st across 1 stitch, ch 2 (does not count as stitch), work 1 hdc in each of (20, 24) hdc, turn work.

Row 8: Ch 2 (does not count as stitch), beginning in first stitch work 1 hdc in each of (20, 23) hdc, turn work, leaving remaining (0, 1) stitch(es) unworked.

Repeat Row 8 working (20, 23) hdc until armhole measures 4½" (11.5 cm) ending with a completed wrong-side row, then continue front following instructions under "Shape Neck (all sizes)."

Shape neck (all sizes)

Row 1 (right side): At armhole edge, ch 2 (does not count as stitch), beginning in first stitch work 1 hdc in each of 13 (14, 16, 16, 18) hdc, turn work, leaving remaining stitches unworked.

Row 2 (wrong side): At neck edge, sl st across first 3 stitches, ch 2 (does not count as stitch), work 1 hdc in each of 10 (11, 13, 13, 15) hdc, turn work.

Row 3: Ch 2 (does not count as stitch), beginning in first stitch work 1 hdc in each of 8 (9, 11, 11, 13) stitches, turn work, leaving remaining stitches unworked.

Row 4: Sl st across 0 (1, 1, 1, 1) stitch(es), ch 2 (does not count as stitch), work 1 hdc in each of 8 (8, 10, 10, 12) stitches, turn work.

Row 5: Ch 2 (does not count as stitch), beginning in first stitch work 1 hdc in each of 8 (8, 10, 10, 12) remaining hdc, turn work.

Repeat Row 5 until front is same length as back. Fasten off.

Right Front (as worn)

Work same as left front to armhole shaping, ending with a completed wrong-side row.

Shape armhole

Row 1 (right side): At center front edge, ch 2 (does not count as stitch), beginning in first stitch work 1 hdc in each of 20 (24, 28, 30, 34) hdc, turn work leaving remaining stitches unworked.

Row 2 (wrong side): At armhole edge, sl st across first 2 (2, 3, 3, 3) stitches, ch 2 (does not count as stitch), work 1 hdc in each 18 (22, 25, 27, 31) hdc, turn work.

Row 3: Ch 2 (does not count as stitch), beginning in first stitch work 1 hdc in each of next 17 (21, 23, 25, 29) hdc, turn work, leaving remaining 1 (1, 2, 2, 2) stitches unworked.

Row 4: Sl st across 0 (1, 1, 2, 2) stitch(es), ch 2 (does not count as stitch), work 1 hdc in each of 17 (20, 22, 23, 27) hdc, turn work.

Row 5: Ch 2 (does not count as stitch), beginning in first stitch work 1 hdc in each of 17 (19, 21, 22, 26) hdc, turn work, leave remaining 0 (1, 1, 1, 1) stitch(es) unworked.

Row 6: Sl st across 0 (0, 1, 1, 1) stitch(es), ch 2 (does not count as stitch), work 1 hdc in each of 17 (19, 20, 21, 25) hdc, turn work.

Row 7: Ch 2 (does not count as stitch), beginning in first stitch work 1 hdc in each of 17 (19, 20, 20, 24) hdc, turn work, leaving remaining 0 (0, 0, 1, 1) stitch(es) unworked.

Sizes XS, S, M only: Repeat Row 7 working 17 (19, 20) hdc until armhole measures 3 (3½, 3½)" [7.5 (9, 9) cm], ending with a wrong-side row completed, then continue front following instructions under "Shape Neck (all sizes)."

Sizes L and XL work as follows:

Row 8: Sl st across (0, 1) stitch(es), ch 2 (does not count as stitch), beginning in same stitch, work 1 hdc in each of (20, 23) hdc, turn work.

Row 9: Ch 2 (does not count as stitch), beginning in first stitch work 1 hdc in each of (20, 23) stitches, turn work.

Repeat Row 9 working (20, 23) hdc until piece measures 4½" (11.5 cm) from beginning of armhole shaping, ending with a completed wrong-side row, then continue front following instructions under "Shape Neck (all sizes)."

Shape neck (all sizes)

Row 1 (right side): At center front edge, sl st across first 4 (5, 4, 4, 5) stitches, ch 2 (does not count as stitch), work 1 hdc in each of 13 (14, 16, 16, 18) hdc, turn work.

Row 2 (wrong side): Ch 2, beginning in first stitch, work 1 hdc in each of 10 (11, 13, 13, 15) hdc, turn work, leaving remaining stitches unworked.

Row 3: Sl st across first 2 stitches, ch 2 (does not count as stitch), work 1 hdc in each of 8 (9, 11, 11, 13) hdc, turn work.

Row 4: Ch 2 (does not count as stitch), beginning in first stitch work 1 hdc in each of 8 (8, 10, 10, 12) hdc, turn work, leaving remaining 0 (1, 1, 1, 1) stitch(es) unworked.

Repeat Row 4 working 8 (8, 10, 10, 12) hdc until right front measures same as Left Front and Back. Fasten off.

Finishing

With right sides of work together, sew side and shoulder seams using either a sl st crochet or backstitch seaming method as shown in Figures 1 and 2.

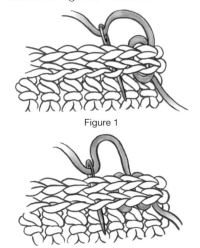

Figure 1

Figure 2

Armhole edge

Row 1: With right side of work facing and beginning at side seam, attach yarn, ch 1, work 50 (54, 54, 58, 58) single crochet evenly around armhole edge, join with sl st to ch 1 at beginning of round. Armhole should lie smooth and flat; if it's too tight, and appears puckered or pulled together, add more single crochet stitches. If the armhole is wavy, reduce the number of single crochet stitches until it's smooth and flat.

Row 2: Ch 1, work 1 single crochet in each single crochet. Fasten off.

Neck edge

With right side of work facing and beginning at front edge, attach yarn, ch 1, work 74 (80, 80, 84, 88) single crochet evenly around neck edge, turn work.

Row 2: Ch 1, work 1 single crochet in each single crochet. Fasten off.

Ruffle at lower edge

With right side of work facing, work 1 single crochet in outer half of each beginning ch for a total of 100 (114, 130, 140, 154) single crochet, turn work.

Row 2: Ch 4 (counts as 1 tr), *work 1 tr in first single crochet, work 2 tr in next single crochet*; repeat from * to * across lower edge to last single crochet, work 2 tr in last single crochet—151 (172, 196, 211, 232) tr. Fasten off.

Left front edge (button band)

With right side of work facing and beginning at neck edge, work 54 (56, 56, 60, 60) single crochet evenly spaced along left front edge between neck edge and the top of ruffle, turn work.

Row 2: Ch 1, work 1 single crochet in each single crochet, turn work.

Repeat Row 2 two more times for a total of 4 rows (including the first row). Fasten off. Using safety pins, mark placement for top and bottom buttons about 1 (2, 2, 4, 4) single crochet from upper and lower edges; evenly space remaining 3 buttons between top and bottom buttons.

Right front edge (buttonhole band)

With right side of work facing, join yarn at top of ruffle and work 54 (56, 56, 60, 60) single crochet evenly spaced along right front edge ending at neckline, turn work. Work band as for button band through first 2 rows.

Row 3: Ch 1, work 1 single crochet in each of first 1 (2, 2, 4, 4) single crochet, *ch 2, skip next 2 single crochet, work 1 single crochet in each of next 10 single crochet, ch 2, skip next 2 single crochet, work 1 single crochet in each of next 11 single crochet*; repeat from * to * one more time, ch 2, skip next 2 single crochet, work 1 single crochet in each of next 1 (2, 2, 4, 4) single crochet, turn work.

Row 4: Ch 1, work 1 single crochet in 1 (2, 2, 4, 4) single crochet, work 1 single crochet in each of next 2 ch, *work 1 single crochet in each of next 11 single crochet, work 1 single crochet in each of next 2 ch, work 1 single crochet in each of next 10 single crochet, work 1 single crochet in each of next 2 ch*; repeat from * to * 1 more time, work 1 single crochet in each of next 1 (2, 2, 4, 4) single crochet. Fasten off.

Sew buttons on button band opposite buttonholes, adjusting pin markers if necessary. Weave in loose ends to wrong side of work. Steam or block to size as needed.

7 Working in Rounds

Now it's time to learn how to work in rounds. Adding this knowledge to your repertoire will allow you to create projects with seamless constructions— a skill that is particularly useful when making hats and bags and tubular shapes, such as the Fingerless Gloves featured in this chapter. Rounds usually begin with a circle but can also, as in the case of the Urban Shopper Tote, begin from a straight chain.

There are a few fundamental differences between working back and forth in rows, as we have done thus far, and working in rounds.

First, you will not be turning your work after every row, so the right side (outside) of the fabric will always be facing you when you work in rounds. Because of this change, your stitches will look slightly different.

Second, there are two ways of moving from one round to the next.

⤳ Joining the last stitch of a round to the beginning of the next round with a slip stitch; then using the appropriate number of chains to get to the stitch height of the next round—the most common method

⤳ Working in what is known as "spiral method," where the work is continuous and one round goes right into the next

The projects in this chapter will help you master both methods.

Finally, it's a good idea in both situations to use a marker (a safety pin or paper clip works well) to designate the beginning of the round. It is easy to get carried away!

Color Block Flash Cap

Flash Caps

Need to know

Gauge (page 35)
Slipknot (page 22)
Chain stitch (page 22)
Turning chain (page 23)
Single crochet (pages 24–25)
Half double crochet
    (pages 26–27)
Fasten off (page 36)
Changing colors (page 32)
Stitch markers (page 13)
Slip stitch (page 30)
Working in rounds (page 33)
Weaving in loose ends
    (page 36)

Abbreviations

ch   chain stitch
hdc   half double crochet
sc   single crochet
sl st   slip stitch

These cute caps fit close to the head and are easily varied to create many hat styles. Even the basic shape can look different just by the way it is colored! Add a few inches (cm) if you want a cuff. A softer fit can be achieved by using a larger hook or, as we have done here, by making a slight change in stitch from single crochet to half double crochet.

Finished Size

Border Stripe Flash Cap and Skinny Stripe Flash Cap
Circumference: 21" (53.5 cm) at lower edge
Length: 7" (18 cm)

Color Block Flash Cap
Circumference: 23" (58.5 cm) at lower edge
Length: 7" (18 cm)

Materials

Yarn: CYCA classification: 4 Medium, Worsted Weight; about 110 yards (101 meters) total for the hdc hat, and 140 yards (128 m) for each single crochet hat.

Shown here: Classic Elite Yarns Flash (100% mercerized cotton; 93 yards [85 meters], 50 grams): #6104 thistle (A), #6168 tangerine (B), #6193 electric blue (C). Border Stripe Flash Cap: 1 skein each B and C. Skinny Stripe Flash Cap: 1 skein each A and B. Color Block Flash Cap: 1 skein each A and C.

Hook: Size H/8 (5 mm). Adjust hook size if necessary to obtain correct gauge.

Notions: Yarn needle, for working in ends; safety pin, to mark round beginning.

Gauge

Size H/8 (5 mm) hook used for the following gauges:
17 single crochet and 20 rounds = 4" (10 cm)
14 half double crochet and 10 rounds = 4" (10 cm)

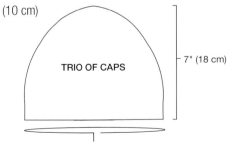

TRIO OF CAPS

7" (18 cm)

Single crochet caps 21" (53.5 cm)
Half double crochet cap 23" (58.5 cm)

Border Stripe Flash Cap (Single Crochet)

Using the hook size needed to obtain correct gauge and color C, ch 4, join with a sl st to form a ring (page 33, Version I, Figure 1).

Round 1: Ch 1 (use safety pin to mark this stitch; move pin at beginning of each round), work 8 sc into center of ring, join with sl st to ch 1 at beginning of round.

Round 2: Ch 1, work 2 sc into each sc, join with sl st to ch 1 at beginning of round—16 sc.

Round 3: Ch 1, *work 2 sc in first sc, work 1 sc in next sc*; repeat from * to * around, join with sl st to ch 1 at beginning of round—24 sc.

Round 4: Ch 1, *work 2 sc in first sc, work 1 sc in each of next 2 sc*; repeat from * to * around, join with sl st to ch 1 at beginning of round—32 sc.

Round 5: Ch 1, *work 2 sc in first sc, work 1 sc in each of next 3 sc*; repeat from * to * around, join with sl st to top of ch 1 at beginning of round—40 sc.

Round 6: Ch 1, work 1 sc in each sc, join with sl st to top of ch 1 at beginning of round.

Round 7: Ch 1, *work 2 sc in first sc, work 1 sc in each of next 4 sc*; repeat from * to * around, join with sl st to top of ch 1 at beginning of round —48 sc.

Round 8: Repeat Round 6.

Round 9: Ch 1, *work 2 sc in first sc, work 1 sc in each of next 5 sc*; repeat from * to * around, join with sl st to top of ch 1 at beginning of round—56 sc.

Round 10: Repeat Round 6.

Round 11: Ch 1, * work 2 sc in first sc, work 1 sc in each of next 6 sc*; repeat from * to * around, join with sl st to top of ch 1 at beginning of round—64 sc.

Round 12: Repeat Round 6.

Round 13: Ch 1, *work 2 sc in first sc, work 1 sc in each of next 7 sc*; repeat from * to * around, join with sl st to top of ch 1 at beginning of round—72 sc.

Round 14: Repeat Round 6.

Round 15: Ch 1, *work 2 sc in first sc, work 1 sc in each of next 8 sc*; repeat from * to * around, join with sl st to top of ch 1 at beginning of round—80 sc.

Round 16: Repeat Round 6.

Round 17: Ch 1, *work 2 sc in first sc, work 1 sc in each of next 9 sc*; repeat from * to * around, join with sl st to top of ch 1 at beginning of round—88 sc. At this point the hat should measure about 21" (53.5 cm) in circumference.

Round 18: Ch 1, work 1 sc in each sc, join with sl st to top of ch 1 at beginning of round.

Repeat Round 18 until hat measures 5" (12.5 cm) tall from center top straight down to bottom edge. Fasten off C. Continuing to work even, attach B at beginning of next round and work 4 rounds. Fasten off B. Attach C and continue to work even in sc until hat measures a total length of 7" (18 cm) tall. Fasten off C.

Skinny Stripe Flash Cap (Single Crochet)

Work as for Border Stripe Cap, except begin with color B and alternate 2 rounds each of B and A throughout until cap measures about 6½" (16.5 cm) in length. Work 1 more round of each color. Finished length is slightly less than 7" (18 cm). Fasten off.

Color Block Flash Cap (Half Double Crochet)

Using the hook size needed to obtain correct gauge and color A, ch 4, join with a sl st to form ring (page 33, Version I, Figure 1).

Round 1: Ch 2, work 10 hdc in ring, join with sl st to top of ch 2 at beginning of round.

Some stitches have a different look when they are worked in the round instead of back and forth. This is the case with single crochet and half double crochet. Compare the effect of single crochet in these caps to that of the scarves in Chapter Four.

Skinny Stripe Flash Cap

Border Stripe *Flash Cap*

Round 2: Ch 2, work 2 hdc in each hdc, join with sl st to top of ch 2 at beginning of round—20 hdc.

Round 3: Ch 2, *work 2 hdc in first hdc, work 1 hdc in next hdc*; repeat from * to * around, join with sl st to top of ch 2 at beginning of round—30 hdc.

Round 4: Ch 2, *work 2 hdc in first hdc, work 1 hdc in each of next 2 hdc*; repeat from * to * around, join with sl st to top of ch 2 at beginning of round—40 hdc.

Round 5: Ch 2, work 1 hdc in each hdc, join with sl st to top of ch 2 at beginning of round. Fasten off A.

Round 6: Attach C, ch 2, *work 2 hdc in first hdc, work 1 hdc in each of next 3 hdc*; repeat from * to * around, join with sl st to top of ch 2 at beginning of round—50 hdc.

Round 7: Ch 2, work 1 hdc in each hdc around, join with sl st to top of ch 2 at beginning of round.

Round 8: Ch 2, *work 2 hdc in first hdc, work 1 hdc in each of next 4 hdc*; repeat from * to * around, join with sl st to top of ch 2 at beginning of round—60 hdc.

Round 9: Repeat Round 7.

Round 10: Ch 2, *work 2 hdc in first hdc, work 1 hdc in each of next 5 hdc*; repeat from * to * around, join with sl st to top of ch 2 at beginning of round—70 hdc.

Round 11: Repeat Round 7.

Round 12: Ch 2, *work 2 hdc in first hdc, work 1 hdc in each of next 6 hdc*; repeat from * to * around, join with sl st to top of ch 2 at beginning of round—80 hdc. Fasten off A.

Round 13: Attach A, ch 2, work 1 hdc in each hdc, join with sl st to top of ch 2.

Repeat Round 13 until cap measures 7" (18 cm) straight down from top of cap. Fasten off A.

Finishing

Weave in loose ends to wrong side with yarn needle.

96

Fingerless Gloves

Need to know

Gauge (page 35)

Winding yarn into center-pull
  ball (below)

Slipknot (page 22)

Chain stitch (page 22)

Slip stitch (page 30)

Single crochet (pages 24–25)

Double crochet (page 28)

Weaving in loose ends
  (page 36)

Fasten off (page 36)

Abbreviations

ch   chain

dc   double crochet

sl st   slip stitch

sc   single crochet

sp   space

Elegant and easy, these little
fingerless gloves are quick to
make and cozy to wear. Pamper
yourself and your friends with a
little bit of luxury.

**Finished Size (to fit
an average woman's
hand)**

Length: 8" (20.5 cm)

Circumference: 8" (20.5 cm)

Materials

Yarn: CYCA classification: 2 Fine, Sport- or
  DK-weight mohair; about 300 yards (275
  meters).

Shown here: Alchemy Yarns of Transformation
  Haiku (60% mohair, 40% silk; 325 yards
  [297 meters], 25 grams): 34W turquoise
  pool, 1 skein.

Hook: Size G/6 (4 mm). Adjust hook size if
  necessary to obtain correct gauge.

Note: This pattern is written in one size. To
  make a slightly smaller glove, use a hook
  one size smaller than the hook size required
  to achieve the recommended gauge. To
  make a larger glove, use a hook one size
  larger than required for gauge.

Notions: Safety pin, to mark rounds; yarn
  needle, to weave in ends.

Gauge

17 stitches and 6 rounds = 3" (7.5 cm) with
  size G/6 (4 mm) hook in pattern stitch using
  2 strands of yarn held together as one.

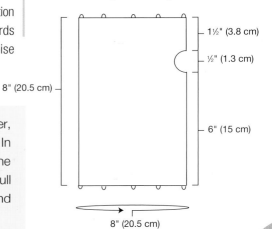

Tip: Only one skein of yarn is required to make both gloves, however,
two strands of yarn are held together as one throughout this project. In
order to achieve this, wind the yarn into two separate balls and hold one
strand from each ball as you work. Or, wind the yarn into a center-pull
ball and work using one strand from the center together with the strand
from the outer edge of the ball (see Tip on page 66).

Gloves (make two)

Note: Glove is worked from top to bottom (fingers to wrist). This project is a slight variation on working in the round. The longer chain is joined to form a loop and the first round is worked into each chain instead of into the center of the loop.

Holding 2 strands together as 1, ch 45, join with sl st to first ch to form ring.

Round 1: Ch 1, place marker, work 1 sc in each ch, join with sl st to beginning ch.

Note: Move marker to first ch at beginning of each subsequent round.

Round 2: Ch 1, work 1 sc in each sc, join with sl st.

Round 3: Repeat Round 2.

Round 4 (begin pattern stitch): Ch 3 (counts as 1 dc), skip next 2 sc, *work (1 dc, ch 1, 1 dc) in next sc, skip 2 sc*; repeat from * to * around, ending with (1 dc, ch 1) in same sc as beginning ch 3, join with sl st to top of beginning ch 3.

Round 5: Ch 3, *skip 2 dc, work (1 dc, ch 1, 1 dc) in next ch-1 sp*; repeat from * to * around ending with (1 dc, ch 1) in same sp as beginning ch 3, join with sl st to top of beginning ch 3.

Round 6 (thumb opening): Work in pattern as established over first 37 stitches, ch 8 loosely, join with sl st to top of beginning ch 3.

Round 7: Ch 3, work in pattern over first 37 stitches, *skip 2 ch, work (1 dc, ch 1, 1 dc) in next ch*; repeat from * to * 1 more time, skip 2 ch, work (1 dc, ch 1) in same sp as beginning ch 3, join with sl st to top of ch 3.

Continue in pattern until glove measures a total length of 7½"
(19 cm). Work 2 rounds in sc. Work 1 round in Picot Edge pattern
stitch. Fasten off.

Finishing

To make a Picot Edge at the beginning of glove, work as follows:
With right side of work facing, attach yarn at joining point of beginning
edge, ch 1, work 1 round in Picot Edge pattern stitch (see Picot Edge
at right) working into outer half of beginning ch, join with sl st to ch 1
at beginning of round. Fasten off. To finish thumb opening, with right
side of work facing, attach yarn at either corner of thumb opening, ch
1, work 1 sc in same sp, work a total of 24 sc evenly spaced around
the thumb opening, join with sl st to beginning ch 1. Fasten off. Weave
in loose ends.

Figure 1

Figure 2

Pattern Stitches

**Open V-Stitch (multiple of 3 stitches
worked in the round)**
Ch a multiple of 3, join work with sl st
into first ch.
Round 1: Ch 4, work 1 dc in same sp
(first ch), *skip 2 ch, work (1 dc, ch 1, 1 dc)
in next ch*; repeat from * to * around, join
with sl st to third ch of beginning ch 4.
Round 2: Ch 3 (counts as 1 dc), *skip 2
dc, work (1 dc, ch 1, 1 dc) in ch-1 sp*;
repeat from * to * around, in last sp work
(1 dc, ch 1), join with sl st to top of beginning ch 3.

Repeat Round 2 for pattern.

**Picot Edge (multiple of 5 stitches
worked in the round)**
Round 1: Ch 1, *work 1 sc in each of
first 4 sc, in next sc work (1 sc, ch 3, 1
sc)*; repeat from * to * around (Figures
1 and 2), join with sl st to beginning ch.
Fasten off.

Farmer's Market Bag

Need to know

Gauge (page 35)

Slipknot (page 22)

Chain stitch (page 22)

Single crochet (pages 24–25)

Double crochet (page 28)

Half double crochet
   (pages 26–27)

Slip stitch (page 30)

Working in rounds (page 33)

Weaving in loose ends
   (page 36)

Abbreviations

ch   chain

hdc   half double crochet

dc   double crochet

sc   single crochet

sl st   slip stitch

sp   space

Large enough to hold a week's worth of produce from the country stand yet small enough to tote a baguette; this lightweight power shopping bag is collapsible and can be folded up small to keep it handy. The linen yarn provides strength without bulk, and the loose stitches keep the bag flexible.

Finished Size

Circumference: about 26½" (67.5 cm)

Length: about 17" (43 cm), excluding handles

Handles: about 18" (45.5 cm) each, in length, untied

Materials

Yarn: CYCA classification: 3, Light Worsted-weight linen, about 500 yards (457 meters).

Shown here: Euroflax Athens (100% wet-spun linen; 200 yards [183 meters], 100 grams): Moss Lake, 3 skeins.

Hook: Size G/6 (4 mm). Adjust hook size if necessary to obtain correct gauge.

Notions: Safety pins, for marking rounds; yarn needle, for weaving in ends.

Gauge

18 stitches and 12 rounds = 4" (10 cm) with size G/6 (4 mm) hook in half double crochet.

Note: This piece is worked in the round in a spiral fashion up to the handles. So instead of joining rounds with a slip stitch, the beginning of the round is marked but worked over. The result is no line where the rounds meet, but the pattern is slightly askew due to the spiral effect. Linen yarn tends to stretch, so the handles are made to knot at the top, allowing for adjustability.

Bag

Ch 4, join with sl st to form ring.

Round 1: Ch 2 (does not count as stitch), work 10 hdc into center of ring—10 hdc. Use safety pin in last stitch to mark the end of round. Move pin at the end of each round.

Round 2: Work 2 hdc in each hdc—20 hdc.

Round 3: *Work 1 hdc in first hdc, work 2 hdc in next hdc*; repeat from * to * around—30 hdc.

Round 4: *Work 1 hdc in each of first 2 hdc, work 2 hdc in next hdc*, repeat from * to * around—40 hdc.

Round 5: *Work 1 hdc in each of first 3 hdc, work 2 hdc in next hdc*; repeat from * to * around—50 hdc.

Round 6: *Work 1 hdc in each of first 4 hdc, work 2 hdc in next hdc*, repeat from * to * around—60 hdc.

Round 7: *Work 1 hdc in each of first 5 hdc, work 2 hdc in next hdc*, repeat from * to * around—70 hdc.

Round 8: *Work 1 hdc in each of first 6 hdc, work 2 hdc in next hdc*; repeat from* to * around—80 hdc.

Round 9: *Work 1 hdc in each of first 7 hdc, work 2 hdc in next hdc*; repeat from * to * around—90 hdc.

Round 10: *Work 1 hdc in each of first 8 hdc, work 2 hdc in next hdc*; repeat from * to * around—100 hdc.

Round 11: *Work 1 hdc in each of first 9 hdc, work 2 hdc in next hdc*; repeat from * to * around—110 hdc.

18" (45.5 cm)

17" (43 cm)

26½" (67.5 cm)

Round 12: *Work 1 hdc in each of first 10 hdc, work 2 hdc in next hdc*; repeat from * to * around—120 hdc.

At this point the crocheted circle should measure about 9¼" (23.5 cm) in diameter and about 28½" (72.5 cm) around.

Rounds 13–16: Work 1 hdc in each hdc.

Begin Mesh pattern

Round 1: *Ch 3, skip 3 hdc, 1 sc in next hdc*; repeat from * to * around.

Round 2: Ch 5, work 1 sc in first ch-3 sp, *ch 5, work 1 sc in next ch-3 sp*; repeat from * to * around.

Round 3: Ch 5, work 1 sc in first ch-5 sp, *ch 5, work 1 sc in next ch-5 sp*; repeat from * to * around.

Rounds 4–19: Repeat Round 3 sixteen more times for a total of 19 rounds (counting from Round 1).

Round 20: *Ch 3, work 1 sc in next ch-5 sp*; repeat from * to * around.

Round 21: *Work 3 hdc in first ch-3 sp, work 1 hdc in next sc*; repeat from * to * around.

Round 22: Work 1 hdc in each hdc—120 hdc.

Rounds 23–27: Repeat Round 22.

Handles (worked flat, back and forth)

Count 60 stitches from beginning marker and place a second safety pin to mark halfway point on bag. With right side facing and beginning where yarn is still attached, work as follows:

Row 1: Ch 2 (does not count as stitch), work 1 hdc in each of next 40 hdc, turn work.

Row 2: Ch 2, work 1 hdc in each of next 35 hdc, turn work.

Row 3: Ch 2, work 1 hdc in each of next 30 hdc, turn work.

Row 4: Ch 2, work 1 hdc in each of next 27 hdc, turn work.

Row 5: Ch 2, work 1 hdc in each of next 24 hdc, turn work.

Row 6: Ch 2, work 1 hdc in each of next 22 hdc, turn work.

Row 7: Ch 2, work 1 hdc in each of next 20 hdc, turn work.

Row 8: Ch 2, work 1 hdc in each of next 19 hdc, turn work.

Row 9: Ch 2, work 1 hdc in each of next 18 hdc, turn work.

Work as for Row 9, working 1 stitch fewer in each row until 12 stitches remain. Work even in hdc on 12 stitches until narrow part of handle measures 11" (28 cm), and about 17½" (44.5 cm) from beginning of handle.

Shape handle top

Row 1: Ch 2, work 1 hdc in each of next 10 hdc, turn work.

Row 2: Ch 2, work 1 hdc in each of next 8 hdc, turn work.

Row 3: Ch 2, work 1 hdc in each of next 6 hdc, turn work.

Row 4: Ch 2, work 1 hdc in each of next 4 hdc. Fasten off.

For second handle, right side of work facing, attach yarn at halfway marker, beginning in the same stitch, repeat handle shaping to match.

Finishing

Weave in loose ends.

Round 1: Attach yarn at left-hand lower edge of either handle and work 1 round in single crochet as follows: ch 1, work 1 sc in same space, *work 1 sc in each of next 20 hdc, work 75 sc along handle curve and edge, work 4 sc across top of handle, work 75 sc along side and curve of handle*; repeat from * to * one more time, join with sl st to top of ch 1 at beginning of round.

Note: It's okay to adjust the number of sc stitches made as you work around the handles. The goal is to keep the handle sides smooth and even and not puckered or ruffled, so add or subtract sc stitches from the numbers given above, if needed.

Round 2: Chain 1, work 1 single crochet in each single crochet, join with slip stitch to top of chain 1, fasten off.

Tie handles together at desired length.

Urban Shopper Tote

Need to know

Gauge (page 35)

Winding yarn into center-pull
   ball (page 97)

Slipknot (page 22)

Chain stitch (page 22)

Single crochet (pages 24–25)

Double crochet (page 28)

Slip stitch (page 30)

Changing colors (page 32)

Marking stitches (page 13)

Working in rounds (page 33)

Weaving in loose ends
   (page 36)

Abbreviations

ch   chain stitch

dc   double crochet

sc   single crochet

sl st   slip stitch

sp   space

This trendy tote is perfect for a trip to the greengrocers or for picking up just a few items anywhere. It rolls up easily to fit in your purse or your pocket and keep handy. This tote is worked in the round but in oval fashion instead of circular. This is achieved by working around a base chain, first working stitches down one side then up the other.

Finished Size

Width: 11" (28 cm)
Length: 13" (33 cm)

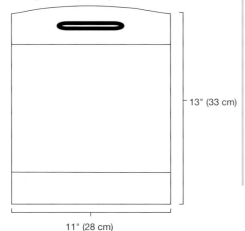

13" (33 cm)

11" (28 cm)

Materials

Yarn: CYCA classification: 2 Sport, used double; about 306 yards (280 meters) main color and 153 yards (140 meters) contrast color.

Shown here: Muench Yarns GGH Safari (78% linen, 22% nylon; 153 yards [140 meters], 50 grams): #30 teal (main color), 2 skeins; #32 coral (contrasting color), 1 skein.

Note: Two strands of yarn are held together as one throughout this project. Wind the yarn into a center-pull ball (if not already prepared this way) and work using one strand from the center together with the strand from the outer edge of the ball.

Hook: Size H/8 (5 mm). Adjust hook size if necessary to obtain correct gauge.

Notions: Yarn needle, for weaving in loose ends; safety pin, to mark round beginning.

Gauge

15 single crochet and 18 rows = 4" (10 cm) with size H/8 (5 mm) hook and 2 strands held together as one.

Note: The bottom edge begins with CC stripe not visible in photo.

Tote

Holding 2 strands together, with contrasting color (CC) loosely ch 41.

Round 1: Starting in second ch from hook work 1 sc in each of first 39 ch, work 3 sc in next ch, rotate work and continue working into other side of ch, work 1 sc in each of next 39 ch, work 2 sc in last ch, join with sl st to beginning stitch. Fasten off.

Round 2: Attach main color (MC), ch 1 and mark with safety pin (move pin to beginning stitch of each round as you progress), work 1 sc in each sc for a total of 83 sc, join with sl st to ch 1 at beginning of round.

Rounds 3–8: Repeat Round 2 six more times.

Begin Openwork

Round 1: Ch 3 (counts as 1 dc), work 1 dc in next sc, ch 2, skip next 2 sc, *work 1 dc in each of next 2 sc, ch 2, skip next 2 sc*; repeat from * to * around, join with sl st to top of beginning ch 3.

Round 2: Ch 5 (counts as 1 dc and 2 ch), *work 2 dc in next ch-2 sp, ch 2*; repeat from * to * around, ending with 1 dc in last ch-2 sp, join with sl st to 3rd chain of beginning ch 5.

Round 3: Ch 3 (counts as 1 dc), work 1 dc in next ch-2 sp, ch 2, *work 2 dc in next ch-2 sp, ch 2*; repeat from * to * around, join with sl st to top of ch 3.

Repeat Rounds 2 and 3 until there are 11 openwork rounds, ending with a completed Round 3, and work measures about 10" (25.5 cm) from beginning of bag.

Top and Handle

Round 1: Ch 1, *work 1 sc in each of first 2 dc, work 2 sc in ch-2 sp*; repeat from * to * around, join with sl st to ch 1. Fasten off MC.

Round 2: Join CC, ch 1, work 1 sc in each sc for a total of 84 sc, join with sl st to beginning ch.

Rounds 3–8: Repeat Round 2 six more times.

Round 9: Ch 1, work 1 sc in each of first 12 sc, ch 18, skip next 18 sc, work 1 sc in each of next 24 sc, ch 18, skip next 18 sc, work 1 sc in each of next 12 sc, join with sl st to beginning ch.

Round 10: Ch 1, work 1 sc in each of first 12 sc, work 1 sc in each of next 18 ch, work 1 sc in each of next 24 sc, work 1 sc in each of next 18 ch, work 1 sc in each of next 12 sc, join with sl st to ch 1.

Rounds 11 and 12: Ch 1, work 1 sc in each sc, join with sl st to beginning ch. Fasten off CC.

Rounds 13 and 14: Attach MC, work 2 more rounds in sc. Fasten off.

Finishing

Attach MC at lower right-hand corner of one handle opening, work 1 sc in same stitch, work 1 sc in each sc around opening, join with sl st to beginning ch. Fasten off. Repeat with second handle opening. Weave in loose ends.

8

Motifs

Now that you know how to work in rounds, your basic knowledge of crochet wouldn't be complete without learning that American icon, the granny square. Along with being just plain fun to work on, this very popular motif is known for its ease and versatility.

The number and kinds of projects you can create by joining together granny squares are endless. Join just a few squares together for a scarf or lots of squares for a full size coverlet or afghan. Granny squares also make excellent garments. Try using them for ponchos, vests, and skirts.

In this chapter, we'll construct two projects using granny squares: the Light and Shadow Blanket and the Messenger Bag. Both projects have an updated contemporary look because of the color schemes I've chosen for them. While you're working on these projects, you'll learn two very important things about motifs that you can then carry on to other projects:

- How repetitive stitches combine to make a motif
- How changes to a motif's color or yarn can change its personality

Motifs are also a very portable way to accomplish a large project. There's no need to carry the workings of an entire blanket with you when you can make it a square at a time.

Once you are comfortable with the granny square, there are many other motifs to try. The principle is the same; only the stitches change.

Let's get going and see what wonderful projects we can create with the no-longer-so-old-fashioned granny square!

Light and Shadow Blanket

Need to know

Gauge (page 35)

Slipknot (page 22)

Chain stitch (page 22)

Turning chain (page 23)

Single crochet (pages 24–25)

Double crochet (page 28)

Half double crochet
(pages 26–27)

Slip stitch (page 30)

Fasten off (page 36)

Whipstitch (page 48)

Weaving in loose ends
(page 36)

Abbreviations

ch   chain stitch

dc   double crochet

hdc   half double crochet

sc   single crochet

sl st   slip stitch

The classic granny square afghan has become an icon of comfort and home, but here we'll give it a contemporary look. Bulky yarn allows you to work up this version quickly. Playing with four values of the three different colors and viewing the blanket on the diagonal takes your eye from night to day and back to night.

Finished Size

About 47" (119.5 cm) square including border

Materials

Yarn: CYCA classification: 6 Super Bulky; about 1,500 yards (1,372 meters).

Shown here: Brown Sheep Lamb's Pride Bulky (85% wool, 15% mohair; 125 yards [114 meters], 113 grams): M75 blue heirloom (I), 3 skeins; M83 raspberry (E), M78 Aztec turquoise (F), M29 Jack's plum (K), M85 ink blue (L), 2 skeins each; M155 lemon drop (A), M38 Lotus pink (B), M57 brite blue (C), M22 autumn harvest (D), M97 rust (G), M23 fuchsia (H), M89 roasted coffee (J), 1 skein each.

Hook: Size K/10½ (6.5 mm). Adjust hook size if necessary to obtain correct gauge.

Notions: Yarn needle, for weaving in loose ends; safety pins.

Gauge

1 motif = 5⅕" (13.2 cm) square with size K/10½ (6.5 mm) hook.

Pattern Stitch

Granny Square Motif
Note: Each motif is made up of three colors. See page 109 for colorway sequences and diagram and key for motif placement (group of colors).

With first color ch 4, join with sl st to form ring (see page 33, Version I, Figure 1).

Round 1: Ch 3 (counts as 1 dc), work 2 dc into ring, (ch 3, work 3 dc into ring) 3 times, ch 3, join with sl st to top of beginning ch 3. Fasten off.

Round 2: Attach second color to any ch-3 space, ch 3 (counts as 1 dc), work (2 dc, ch 3, 3 dc) into same space, (ch 1, [into next ch-3 sp work 3 dc, ch 3, 3 dc]) 3 times, ch 1, join with sl st to top of beginning ch 3. Fasten off.

Round 3: Attach third color to any ch-3 space, ch 3 (counts as 1 dc), work (2 dc, ch 3, 3 dc) into same space, (ch 1, work 3 dc into next ch-1 space, ch 1, work [3 dc, ch 3, 3 dc] into next ch-3 space) 3 times, ch 1, work 3 dc into next ch-1 space, ch 1, join with sl st to top of beginning ch 3. Fasten off.

Blanket
Make 64 motifs divided as follows: 8 Motif I, 26 Motif II, 18 Motif III, 12 Motif IV. Weave in loose ends. Using whipstitch and yarn to match the dominant edge color (this will change from area to area), assemble motifs according to the assembly diagram.

Border
Round 1: Starting at any corner with right side of work facing, attach first color (blue heirloom), ch 1, work 1 sc in each dc or ch, work 2 sc in each corner stitch (the corner stitch is the last stitch on a side and the first stitch on the next side, so you will have two stitches side by side with two stitches worked in each one), mark each corner with a safety pin, join with sl st to beginning ch 1. This works out to 15 sc per square or 120 sc per side of blanket for a total of 480 sc.

Round 2: Ch 2, work 1 hdc in each sc, working 2 hdc in each corner stitch and moving markers accordingly, join with sl st to top of ch 2. Fasten off.

Round 3: Attach second color (ink blue), work as for Round 2. Fasten off.

Round 4: Attach third color (Jack's plum), ch 1, work 1 sc in each hdc, working 2 sc in each corner stitch, join with sl st to beginning ch 1. Fasten off.

Finishing
Weave in loose ends. Steam or block to size.

Motif I
First color: lemon drop (A)
Second color: Lotus pink (B)
Third color: brite blue (C)

Motif II
First color: autumn harvest (D)
Second color: raspberry (E)
Third color: Aztec turquoise (F)

Motif III
First color: rust (G)
Second color: fuchsia (H)
Third color: blue heirloom (I)

Motif IV
First color: roasted coffee (J)
Second color: Jack's plum (K)
Third color: ink blue (L)

Border
First color: blue heirloom (I)
Second color: ink blue (L)
Third color: Jack's plum (K)

I	Motif I—Colors A, B, C
II	Motif II—Colors D, E, F
III	Motif III—Colors G, H, I
IV	Motif IV—Colors J, K, L

BORDER							
I	II	II	III	III	IV	IV	IV
II	I	II	II	III	III	IV	IV
II	II	I	II	II	III	III	IV
III	II	II	I	II	II	III	III
III	III	II	II	I	II	II	III
IV	III	III	II	II	I	II	II
IV	IV	III	III	II	II	I	II
IV	IV	IV	III	III	II	II	I

BORDER (left) · BORDER (right) · BORDER (bottom)

47" (119.5) — vertical

47" (119.5) — horizontal

Messenger Bag

Need to know

Gauge (page 35)

Slipknot (page 22)

Chain stitch (page 22)

Turning chain (page 23)

Single crochet (pages 24–25)

Double crochet (page 28)

Slip stitch (page 30)

Fasten off (page 36)

Whipstitch (page 48)

Weaving in loose ends
(page 36)

Changing colors (page 32)

Abbreviations

ch   chain stitch

dc   double crochet

sc   single crochet

sl st slip stitch

Constructed from traditional granny squares, this retro-inspired bag looks contemporary once again. Wear it crisscrossed over the shoulder and landing at the hip. The adjustable strap allows for a personal fit.

Finished Size

Back and Front: About 12" (30.5 cm) wide, 11" (28 cm) long (including side and bottom panel)

Flap: About 10 × 10" (25.5 x 25.5 cm) square

Materials

Yarn: CYCA classification: 3 Light Worsted; about 600 yards (549 meters) total.

Shown here: Rowan All Seasons Cotton (60% cotton, 40 % acrylic; 98 yards [90 meters], 50 grams): #213 military (main color), 3 balls; #211 black currant (A), #214 fern (B), and #218 pansy (C), 1 ball each.

Hook: Size E/4 (3.5 mm). Adjust hook size if necessary to obtain the correct gauge.

Note: To create a sturdier fabric, this bag is worked with a smaller hook than this yarn would usually require.

Notions: Yarn needle, for sewing together and weaving in loose ends; 1 pair of 1½" (3.8 cm) D rings; safety pins.

Gauge

16 sc and 16 rows = 4" (10 cm) with size E/4 (3.5 mm) hook; 1 completed Granny Square Motif = 4½" (11.5 cm) square, worked on E/4 (3.5 mm) hook.

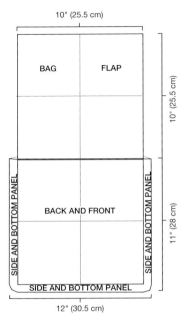

10" (25.5 cm)

| BAG | FLAP |

10" (25.5 cm)

SIDE AND BOTTOM PANEL

BACK AND FRONT

SIDE AND BOTTOM PANEL

11" (28 cm)

SIDE AND BOTTOM PANEL

12" (30.5 cm)

1½" (3.8 cm) SHORT STRAP

6" (15 cm)

1½" (3.8 cm) LONG STRAP

43" (109 cm)

Granny Square Motif

With C, ch 4; join with sl st to form ring (page 33, Version I, Figure 1).

Round 1: With C, ch 3 (counts as 1 dc); work 2 dc into ring, *ch 3, work 3 dc into ring*; repeat from * to * 2 more times, ch 3, join with sl st to top of beginning ch 3. Fasten off.

Round 2: Attach A to any ch-3 space, ch 3 (counts as 1 dc), work (2 dc, ch 3, 3 dc) into same space, *ch 1, work (3 dc, ch 3, 3 dc) in next space*; repeat from * to * 2 more times, ch 1, join with sl st to top of beginning ch 3. Fasten off.

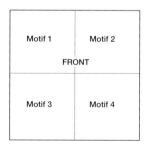

Motif 1	Motif 2
FLAP	
Motif 3	Motif 4
Motif 5	Motif 6
BACK	
Motif 7	Motif 8

Motif 1	Motif 2
FRONT	
Motif 3	Motif 4

Round 3: Attach B to any ch-3 space, ch 3 (counts as 1 dc), work (2 dc, ch 3, 3 dc) in same space, *ch 1, work 3 dc in next ch-1 space, ch 1, work (3 dc, ch 3, 3 dc) into next ch-3 space*; repeat from * to * 2 more times, ch 1, work 3 dc into ch-1 space, ch 1, join with sl st to top of beginning ch 3. Fasten off.

Round 4: Attach main color (MC) to any ch-3 space, ch 3 (counts as 1 dc), work (2 dc, ch 3, 3 dc) into same space, *(ch 1, work 3 dc in next ch-1 space) 2 times, ch 1, work (3 dc, ch 3, 3 dc) in next ch-3 space*; repeat from * to * 2 more times, work (ch 1, 3 dc in next ch 1 space) 2 times, ch 1, join with sl st to top of beginning ch 3. Fasten off.

Bag Front, Back, and Flap

Make 12 motifs. Using whipstitch and MC, join squares into one 4-square piece for Front, and one 8-square piece for Back and Flap (see diagram). Beginning with MC in any corner space of 4-square piece, ch 3 (counts as 1 dc), work 1 dc in same space, work 1 dc in each dc and in each space (18 dc per side of each motif), work 2 dc in each ch-3 space (at motif joins), and work 3 dc in ch-3 spaces at corners of joined pieces, join with sl st to top of beginning ch 3. Repeat for 8-square rectangle.

Side and Bottom Panel

With MC, ch 113.

Row 1: Work 1 sc in second ch from hook and 1 sc in each ch—112 sc. Fasten off.

Rows 2 and 7: Join B, ch 1, 1 sc in each sc across row. Fasten off.

Rows 3 and 6: Join A, repeat Row 2.

Rows 4 and 5: Join C, repeat Row 2.

Row 8: Join MC, repeat Row 2. Fasten off.

Strap (Made in 2 pieces)

Short section: With MC, ch 25.

Row 1: Work 1 sc in second ch from hook and 1 sc in each ch—24 sc.

Row 2: Ch 1, work 1 sc in each sc across row.

Continuing in MC, repeat Row 2 four more times. Fasten off.

Long section: With MC, ch 173.

Work as for short section on 172 stitches. Fasten off.

Finishing

Weave in loose ends being careful to work colors back into themselves. Using safety pins, pin long edge of side and bottom panel to 3 sides of front. Using MC threaded on yarn needle, whipstitch one long edge of panel to front sides and bottom. Repeat with other long edge of side and bottom panel, whipstitching the panel to back and leaving the top flap free (see schematic, page 111). Sew the short edge of the long strap to left hand side of bag (as bag front faces you), placing the short edge about ½" (1.3 cm) down from bag opening, and stitching on the outside of bag. Repeat the sewing process with short strap on the right-hand side. Slip D rings on to opposite end of long strap and fold end under about ¾" (2 cm), sew securely in place. Pull short strap through D rings and adjust for length. With right side of work facing, attach B at right-hand side edge of flap at the bag opening (this will be the right-hand side of flap as the work faces you), work 1 sc in same space then work 1 sc in each dc around the outer edge of the flap, and working 3 sc in each corner dc. Fasten off. Turn bag around so front faces you, attach B to front bag opening at right-hand edge of front, work 1 sc in each dc across. Fasten off. Weave in loose ends.

9

Getting Edgy

This chapter is all about ruffles and flourishes. Not only can you add decorative edges and borders to your crochet projects, you can also embellish just about anything you can get a needle through! The edges on the tanks, clutch, shrug, and foot thongs—all found in this chapter—are widely varied in style and represent only a small sample of what is possible.

As you're working through these projects, you'll pick up two new skills—one creative and one practical:

↝ how to think in three dimensions
↝ how to attach edgings

For fun, make some floral and leaf motifs. They work up quickly and they can be stitched directly to a garment or sewed to pin backs for one-of-a-kind jewelry. What a dashing way to round out your newfound crocheting skills!

Fancy Foot Thongs

Need to know

Gauge (page 35)
Slipknot (page 22)
Chain stitch (page 22)
Turning chain (page 23)
Single crochet (pages 24–25)
Double crochet (page 28)
Slip stitch (page 30)
Fasten off (page 36)
Weaving in ends (page 36)

Abbreviations

ch   chain
dc   double crochet
sc   single crochet
sl st   slip stitch

These foot thongs are a fun way to dress up the barefoot look and show off a pedicure. Based on a triangular motif, they work up in no time.

Finished Size

(fits the average adult female foot)
Width: About 4" (10 cm)
Length: About 4" (10 cm) with 14" (35.5 cm) long ties

Materials

Yarn: CYCA classification: 1 Fingering; about 60 yards (55 meters).

Shown here: Coats and Clark Aunt Lydia's Fashion Crochet Thread (100% mercerized cotton; 150 yards [137 meters] per ball): #0006 Scarlett, 1 ball.

Hook: Size B/1 (2.25 mm). Adjust hook size if necessary to obtain correct gauge.

Notions: Yarn needle, for weaving in loose ends; 4 wooden beads about ½" (1.3 cm) in diameter with large holes; 8 metal-finish beads about ½" (1.3 cm) in diameter with large holes.

Gauge

1 motif (before edge finish) = 3½" (9 cm) long by 3½" (9 cm) wide at longest and widest points with size B/1 (2.25 mm) hook.

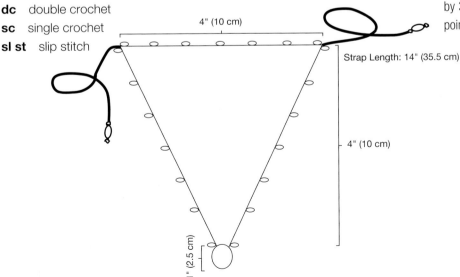

4" (10 cm)

Strap Length: 14" (35.5 cm)

4" (10 cm)

1" (2.5 cm)

Motif

Lace Triangle Motif (make 2 the same)

Ch 6, join with sl st to form ring (page 33, Version I, Figure 1).

Round 1: Ch 1, work 12 sc into ring, join with sl st to beginning ch 1.

Round 2: Ch 10 (counts as 1 dc and ch-7 arch), skip first 2 sc, *work 1 dc in next sc, ch 3, skip 1 sc, work 1 dc in next sc, ch 7, skip 1 sc*; repeat from * to * 1 more time, work 1 dc in next sc, ch 3, skip last sc, join with sl st to third ch of beginning ch 10.

Round 3: Ch 3 (counts as 1 dc), into next ch-7 arch work (3 dc, ch 7, 4 dc), *work 3 dc into next ch-3 space, work (4 dc, ch 7, 4 dc) into next ch-7 arch*; repeat from * to * 1 more time, work 3 dc into last ch-3 space, join with sl st to top of beginning ch 3.

Round 4: Ch 6 (counts as 1 dc and 1 ch-3 space), *work (4 dc, ch 5, 4 dc) in next ch-7 arch, ch 3, skip 2 dc, work 1 dc in next dc, ch 3, skip 2 dc, work 1 sc in next dc, ch 3**, skip 2 dc, work 1 dc into next dc, ch 3*; repeat from * to * 1 more time and then from * to **; sl st to third ch of beginning ch 6. Fasten off.

Picot Trim and Ties

Round 1: Attach yarn to any ch-5 space, ch 1, into same space work (4 sc, ch 16 [for toe loop], 4 sc), *make picot (to make picot, ch 3, sl st into first ch), work 1 sc in each of next 4 dc, make picot, work 3 sc in next ch-3 space, work 1 sc in next dc, make picot, work 3 sc in next ch-3 space, work 1 sc in next sc, make picot, work 3 sc in next ch-3 space, work 1 sc in next dc, make picot, work 3 sc in next ch-3 space, make picot, work 1 sc in each of next 4 dc, make picot**, in ch-5 space work (4 sc, ch 100, starting in second chain from hook work 1 sl st in each ch [for tie], 4 sc)*; repeat from * to * one more time, then from * to **. Fasten off.

Finishing

Weave in loose ends. On each tie, string (1 metal, 1 wooden, 1 metal) bead, tie knot at end of tie to hold beads in place. To wear, slip toe loop over second toe, wrap ties around ankle, and tie in front.

Bobble Clutch Purse

Need to know

Gauge (page 35)

Slipknot (page 22)

Chain stitch (page 22)

Turning chain (page 23)

Single crochet (pages 24–25)

Reverse single crochet
  (page 119)

Double crochet (page 28)

Fasten off (page 36)

Slip stitch (page 30)

Weaving in loose ends
  (page 36)

Abbreviations

ch   chain

dc   double crochet

rev sc   reverse single
  crochet

sc   single crochet

sl st   slip stitch

Edged in a contrasting color using a decorative stitch known as reverse single crochet (sometimes called shrimp or crab stitch or backward crochet), this highly textured purse has a retro feel to it. The bobble stitches are easy and fun to work and create a bold fabric.

Finished Size

Width: 12" (30.5 cm)

Length: 5" (12.5 cm)

Depth: 2.75" (7 cm)

Materials

Yarn: CYCA classification: 4 Worsted Weight, a tape-style yarn; about 450 yards (411 meters).

Shown here: Muench String of Pearls (70% cotton, 20% rayon, 10% polyester; 99 yards [90 meters], 50 grams): #4014 burnt orange (main color), 4 balls; color #4019 magenta (contrasting color), 1 ball.

Hook: Size H/8 (5 mm). Adjust hook size if necessary to obtain correct gauge.

Notions: 1 toggle button about 2" (5 cm) long; yarn needle, for weaving in loose ends; safety pins, to hold pieces together for sewing.

Gauge

15 stitches = 4" (10 cm), 5 rows = 2" (5 cm) with size H/8 (5 mm) hook in pattern stitch.

16 stitches and 16 rows = 4" (10 cm) with size H/8 (5 mm) hook in single crochet.

Main Piece (Front, Back, Flap)

Note: Bobbles are worked on wrong-side rows and then protrude to the right side of the work. If a bobble becomes inverted, poke into it with your little finger or the blunt end of the crochet hook, so it pops out on the right side.

With main color (MC) loosely ch 47.

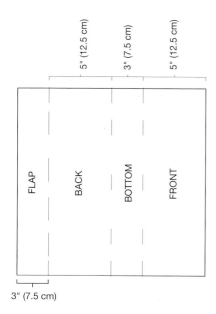

5" (12.5 cm)   3" (7.5 cm)   5" (12.5 cm)

FLAP   BACK   BOTTOM   FRONT

3" (7.5 cm)

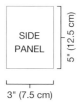

SIDE PANEL

5" (12.5 cm)

3" (7.5 cm)

Row 1 (wrong side): Beginning in second ch from hook work 1 sc in each ch to end of row, turn work—46 sc.

Row 2 (right side): Ch 1, work 1 sc in each sc.

Row 3 (bobble row): Ch 1, work 1 sc in each of first 2 sc stitches, *work 1 sc in each of next 2 sc, wrap yarn over hook, insert hook into next sc (wrap yarn, draw loop through same stitch [3 loops on hook], wrap yarn, draw through first 2 loops on hook) 5 times (there are now 6 loops on hook), wrap yarn over hook, draw through all 6 loops*; repeat from * to * to last 2 stitches, work 1 sc in each of last 2 sc, turn work.

Row 4: Ch 1, work 1 sc in each sc to end of row, turn work.

Row 5 (bobble row): Ch 1, *work 1 sc in each of first 2 sc, wrap yarn over hook, insert hook into next sc, (wrap yarn, draw loop through same stitch, wrap yarn, draw through first 2 loops on hook) 5 times, wrap yarn over hook, draw through all 6 loops*; repeat from * to * to last 4 stitches, work 1 sc in each stitch, turn work.

Row 6: Repeat Row 4.

Continue in pattern stitch repeating Rows 3–6 until main piece measures a total length of 15½" (39.5 cm) ending with a completed wrong side (bobble) row, turn work.

Buttonhole Row: Ch 1, work 1 sc in each of first 21 sc, ch 4, skip next 4 sc, work 1 sc in each of next 21 sc, turn work.

Next Row: Ch 1, work 1 sc in each of first 21 sc, work 1 sc in each of next 4 ch, work 1 sc in each of next 21 sc. Fasten off.

Side Panels (make 2)

With contrasting color (CC), loosely ch 13.

Row 1: Starting in second ch from hook, work 1 sc in each ch to end of row, turn work—12 sc.

Row 2: Ch 1, work 1 sc in each sc, turn work.

Repeat Row 2 until piece measures 5" (12.5 cm). Fasten off.

Finishing

Weave in loose ends. Using safety pins, mark side edges of Main Piece 5" (12.5 cm) up from front edge, 3" (7.5 cm) up from first marker, then 5" (12.5 cm) from second marker (see diagram). Pin one Side Panel to Main Piece, matching corners to safety pins. Remainder of Main Piece will become the front flap. With Main Piece facing and working through edge stitches of both Main Piece and Side Panel, work 18 sc evenly along side edge, 10 sc evenly along bottom edge, and 18 stitches up remaining side edge. Ch 1, do not turn work, work 1 rev sc in each sc. Fasten off. Repeat for second side of bag. Attach CC at right-hand corner of Front edge, ch 1, work 1 sc in each ch (46 sc), skip stitches on side panel, work 10 sc evenly along side of flap, work 1 extra stitch in corner, work 1 sc in each sc along flap edge (46 sc), work 1 extra stitch in corner, work 10 sc evenly spaced along side edge of flap, skip stitches on side panel, join with sl st to beginning ch 1, do not turn work. Ch 1, work 1 rev sc in each sc. Fasten off. Thread yarn needle with CC and tack top side edges of Side Panel together to make a pleat. Sew button on Front to match buttonhole on flap.

Reverse Single Crochet

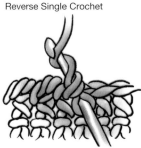

Figure 1: Working from left to right, insert crochet hook into first st, ch1, *insert hook into next st to the right, catch the yarn and draw up a loop through the stitch and under, but not through, the loop on the hook.

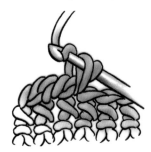

Figure 2: Yarn over hook again, and draw up a loop through both loops on hook*; repeat instructions from * to * to end.

Lacy Shrug

Need to know

Gauge (page 35)

Slipknot (page 22)

Chain stitch (page 22)

Single crochet (pages 24–25)

Double crochet (page 28)

Decrease (page 31)

Stitch markers (page 13)

Fasten off (page 36)

Backstitch (page 90)

Weaving in loose ends
  (page 36)

Blocking (page 36)

Abbreviations

ch   chain stitch

dc   double crochet

sc   single crochet

The edges on this retro-inspired little shrug are an exaggeration of the pattern stitch within. Although it looks elaborate, the pattern stitch is easy to learn and works up quickly.

Finished Size

Width: 46" (117 cm) from cuff to cuff, including border

Length: 25" (63.5 cm) at center back, including border

Materials

Yarn: CYCA classification: 4 Worsted, worsted-weight cotton blend; about 920 yards (841 meters).

Shown here: Cascade Yarns Sierra (80% pima cotton, 20% wool; 191 yards [175 meters], 100 grams): #26 (blue), 5 skeins.

Hook: Size H/8 (5 mm), J/10 (6 mm), K/10½ (6.5 mm). Adjust hook sizes if necessary to obtain correct gauge.

Notions: Yarn needle, for weaving in loose ends and sewing seams; open ring stitch marker.

Gauge

19 stitches = 4¾" (12 cm), 4 stitches = 1" (2.5 cm), and 5 rows = 2" (5 cm) with size H/8 (5 mm) hook in pattern stitch (Arcade Stitch).

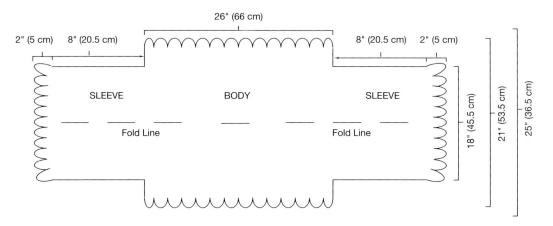

Pattern Stitch (Arcade Stitch)

Ch a multiple of 6 stitches + 1.

Row 1: Work 1 sc in second ch from hook, *ch 3, skip next 3 ch, work 1 sc in each of next 3 ch*; repeat from * to * across, ending with 1 sc in each of last 2 ch, turn work.

Row 2: Ch 1, skip first sc, *skip 1 sc, work 5 dc in ch-3 space, skip 1 sc, work 1 sc in next sc (the center of the 3 sc)*; repeat from * to * across, ending with 1 sc in ch 1 of previous row, turn work.

Row 3: Ch 3, skip (1 sc, 1 dc), *work 1 sc in each of next 3 dc (the center 3 dc of 5 dc), ch 3, skip [1 dc, 1 sc, 1 dc]*; repeat from * to * across, to last group, ending with 1 sc in each of 3 dc, ch 2, skip 1 dc, work 1 sc in ch 1, turn work.

Row 4: Ch 3, skip first sc, work 2 dc in ch-2 space, *skip 1 sc, work 1 sc in next sc (the center sc of 3), skip 1 sc, work 5 dc in the ch-3 space*; repeat from * to * across, ending with 3 dc in last ch-3 space, turn work.

Row 5: Ch 1, skip first dc, work 1 sc in next dc, *ch 3, skip [1 dc, 1 sc, 1 dc], work 1 sc in each of next 3 dc (the center 3 dc of 5 dc)*; repeat from * to *, ending with 1 sc in last dc and 1 sc in top of ch 3, turn work.

Repeat Rows 2–5 for pattern.

Shrug

Starting at sleeve edge loosely ch 73. Beginning with Row 1 of Arcade Stitch, work in pattern on 72 stitches until piece measures 8" (20.5 cm) from beginning ending with a Row 5 completed, turn work.

Shape body as follows: Ch 7 at beginning of next row (Row 2), working into these new chains, 1 sc in second ch from hook, skip next 2 ch, work 5 dc in next ch, skip 2 ch, resume pattern as established for Row 2, starting with 1 sc in end stitch and then repeat Row 2 from * to end of row, turn work—78 stitches.

Next Row: Ch 7, starting with fourth ch from hook work 1 sc in each of next 3 ch, ch 3, resume pattern for Row 3 repeating instructions in pattern from * to end of row—84 stitches. Place open ring marker in last stitch. Don't move marker from this stitch. Work even in pattern stitch on 84 stitches until wide part of piece measures 26" (66 cm) from marker, ending with Row 3.

Decrease for second sleeve: Work in pattern for Row 4 as established to last ch-3 space, work 3 dc in ch-3 space, leaving remaining stitches unworked, turn work.

Next row: Ch 1, work 1 sc in second dc, ch 3, continue in pattern as established for Row 5 to last full scallop, work 1 sc in both second and third dc, turn work—72 stitches (stitch count includes ch-3 groups). Continue in pattern as established until sleeve measures 8" (20.5 cm) ending with a Row 3 or Row 5. (If you finished this sleeve with Row 3, the edging begins with Row 4 of Arcade pattern. If you finished with Row 5, the edging begins with Row 2.)

Sleeve edging (current sleeve): Change to size J/10 (6 mm) hook and work Row 2 or 4 and continue in pattern, turn work. Change hook to size K/10½ (6.5 mm) and work next row (Row 3 or Row 5), turn work. Work 1 more row (Row 4 or Row 2) but work 7 dc in each ch-3 arch (instead of 5 dc) and work 4 dc (instead of 3 dc) in end arches. Fasten off.

Sleeve edging (first sleeve): When you work the edging on this sleeve, the pattern stitches will arch in the opposite direction from those in the rest of the shrug. With right side of work facing, join yarn in first ch at ch edge. With size J/10 (6 mm) hook, work Row 2 across the chain edge, counting the chains as if they were Row 1 of pattern, turn work.

Change hook to size K/10½ (6.5 mm) and work next row (Row 3), turn work. Work 1 more row (Row 4) but work 7 dc in each ch-3 arch (instead of 5 dc) and work 4 dc (instead of 3 dc) in end arches. Fasten off.

Finishing

Remove marker. Fold shrug in half lengthwise and sew sleeve/side seam including edging using a backstitch.

Body Edge (worked the same for both top and bottom edges): With size H/8 (5 mm) hook ch 1, then work 84 sc evenly along edge from seam to seam, turn work. Work Row 1 of Arcade Pattern, turn work. Change to size J/10 (6 mm) hook and work Row 2 of pattern, turn work. Change to size K/10½ (6.5 mm) hook and work Row 3 of pattern, turn work. Work Row 4 of pattern but work 7 dc in each ch-3 arch and 4 dc (instead of 3 dc) in partial arches at edges. Fasten off. Repeat for opposite side of opening. Weave in loose ends. Steam or block lightly.

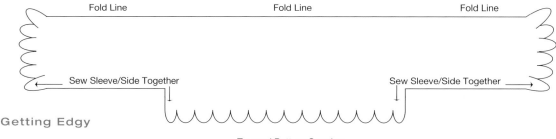

Trim A Tank

Need to know

Gauge (page 35)

Slipknot (page 22)

Chain stitch (page 22)

Turning chain (page 23)

Single crochet (pages 24–25)

Forming a ring (page 33)

Double crochet (page 28)

Treble crochet (page 29)

Stitch markers (page 13)

Blanket stitch (page 124)

Slip stitch (page 30)

Fasten off (page 36)

Weaving in loose ends
    (page 36)

Abbreviations

ch   chain stitch

dc   double crochet

sc   single crochet

sl st   slip stitch

tr   treble crochet

It's fun and easy to personalize a garment. This trio of tank tops represents only a suggestion of the possibilities. You could just as easily trim a T-shirt, a camisole, or a hat. In truth, you can trim just about anything you can get a needle into! Pick a trim to take a garment from plain to fancy in no time. Choose the motifs that appeal to you. Use many or just a few. The statement you make is totally yours—and one-of-a-kind.

Materials

Yarn: CYCA classification: 1 Super Fine, cotton crochet yarn, size 3; 150 yards (137 m) of each color will make the edgings and motifs as shown for more than 3 tops.

Shown here: Aunt Lydia's Fashion Crochet Thread, size 3 (100% mercerized cotton; 150 yards [137 meters] per ball): #264 lime (A), #325 tangerine (B), #625 sage (C), #775 warm rose (D), #65 warm teal (E), 1 ball each.

Tank Top #1: Colors A, B, C

Tank Top #2: Colors A, B, C, D, E

Tank Top #3: Colors B, C, E

Hook: Size B/1 (2.25 mm). Adjust hook size if necessary to obtain correct gauge.

Notions: White cotton tank top; white embroidery floss; sharp sewing needle (with eye large enough to accommodate 3 strands of floss); pins; pin backs (optional); yarn needle, for working in loose ends; stitch marker if making leaf.

Gauge

19 single crochet and 19 rows = 4" (10 cm) with size B/1 (2.25 mm) hook.

Blanket Stitch

Figure 1

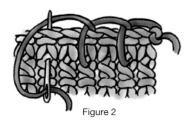

Figure 2

Garment Prep (for all tanks)

Cut a length of embroidery floss to about 36" (91.5 cm) long or a comfortable length for sewing. Divide into two 3-strand sections. Thread the sharp needle with one section; save the other section to use when the first runs out. Beginning at center back neck edge of tank, embroider one row of blanket stitch (Figure 1) around neck edge, placing stitches about ¼" (6 mm) apart (Figure 2). Fasten off with a barrel knot on the wrong side of the garment as follows: Insert needle under the last blanket stitch, wrap the embroidery thread around the needle point 3 times, pull the needle through the wraps slowly and tighten the wraps into a knot. Hide the thread end by weaving needle and thread between the two layers of garment fabric (neckline facing) for an inch (cm) or so. Exit needle from fabric, pull gently on thread, cut, and allow the end to disappear back into the fabric.

Borders and Motifs

Border #1

Worked over a multiple of 6 stitches.

Round 1: Ch 1, work 1 sc in each blanket stitch, adjusting as necessary to obtain a multiple of 6 stitches, join with sl st to beginning ch 1.

Round 2: Ch 1, *work 1 sc in first sc, skip next 2 sc, work 5 dc in next sc, skip next 2 sc*; repeat from * to * around, join with sl st to beginning ch 1. Fasten off.

Border #2

Worked over a multiple of 3 stitches.

Round 1: Ch 1, work 1 sc in each blanket stitch, adjusting as necessary to obtain a multiple of 3 stitches, join with sl st to beginning ch 1.

Round 2: *Ch 3, skip 2 sc, work 1 sc in next sc*; repeat from * to * around, join with sl st to beginning ch 1. Fasten off.

Border #3

Worked over a multiple of 8 stitches + 1.

Round 1: Ch 1, work 1 sc in each blanket stitch, adjusting as necessary to obtain a multiple of 8 stitches + 1, join with sl st to
beginning ch 1.

Round 2: Ch 3 (counts as 1 dc), work 2 dc in first sc, *chain
3, skip next 3 sc, work 1 sc in next sc, ch 3, skip 3 sc,
work 3 dc in next sc*; repeat from * to * around, ch 3,
join with sl st to top of beginning ch 3. Fasten off.

Motif #1: Clover Leaf

Note: To work 3 tr together work first tr omitting final step and leaving
2 loops on hook, work the next 2 tr the same way, leaving 2 loops
on the hook for each tr worked, then wrap yarn around hook and
pull through all 6 remaining loops.

Ch 5, join with sl st to form circle.

Round 1: Ch 1, work 10 sc into ring, sl st to beginning ch 1.
Round 2: Ch 1, work 1 sc in first sc, *ch 4, work 3 tr together (see
Note above) working first tr in same space as last sc and next 2
tr in each of next 2 sc, ch 4, work 1 sc in same stitch as last tr,
work 1 sc in next sc*; repeat from * to * three more times; *make
stalk:* ch 7, turn, work 1 sc in second ch from hook, then work
1 sc in each of next 5 chains, join with sl st to ch 1 at beginning
of round. Fasten off.

Motif #2: Small Flower

Ch 4, join with sl st to form ring.

Tank 3

Tank 2

Tank 1

Round 1: Ch 1, work 16 sc into ring, join with sl st to beginning ch 1.

Round 2: *Ch 3, work 1 dc in each of next 2 sc, ch 3, work 1 sl st in next sc*; repeat from * to * 4 more times to end of round. Fasten off.

Motif #3: Large Two-Tone Flower

With first color (we used color E) ch 4, join with sl st to form ring.

Round 1: Ch 1, work 16 sc into ring, join with sl st to beginning ch 1. Fasten off.

Round 2: Attach second color (we used color B), *ch 12, work 1 sl st into next sc*; repeat from * to * around. Fasten off.

Motif #4: Leaf

Ch 9.

Row 1: Starting in second ch from hook work 1 sc in each of next 7 ch, work 3 sc in end ch, place marker in middle sc of these 3 sc to mark as end stitch, rotate ch and work 1 sc in opposite side of ch in each of next 7 sc, turn work.

Row 2: Ch 1, skip first sc, work 1 sc in each of next 7 sc, remove marker and work 3 sc in end sc, re-insert marker into new center stitch, work 1 sc in each of next 5 sc, turn work.

Row 3: Ch 1, skip first sc, work 1 sc in each of next 5 sc, remove marker, work 3 sc in next sc (end stitch), re-insert marker into new center stitch, work 1 sc in each of next 5 sc, turn work.

Row 4: Ch 1, skip first sc, work 1 sc in each of next 5 sc, remove marker, work 3 sc in next sc (end stitch), re-insert marker into new center stitch, work 1 sc in each of next 3 sc, turn work.

Row 5: Ch 1, skip first sc, work 1 sc in each of next 3 sc, remove marker, work 3 sc in next sc (end stitch), work 1 sc in each of next 3 sc. Fasten off.

Tank #1

Beginning at either shoulder seam, tie color A to first blanket stitch, work Border #1 around neck edge. Make one Motif #1 in each of colors A, B, and C—3 motifs total. Weave in loose ends on border and motifs. Using 1 strand of embroidery floss and sharp needle, sew motifs to tank, placing evenly around front neck edge.

Tank #2

Beginning at either shoulder seam, tie color D to first blanket stitch, work Border #2 around neck edge. Make one Motif #2 in each of colors A, B, C, D, E—5 motifs total. Weave in loose ends on border and motifs. Using 1 strand of embroidery floss and sharp needle, sew motifs to tank along upper front.

Tank #3

Beginning at either shoulder seam, tie color E to first blanket stitch, work Border #3 around neck edge. Make one Motif #3 using color E as the first color, and B as second color. Make two of Motif #4 using color C. Weave in loose ends on border and motifs. Arrange all three motif pieces on left chest and sew into place using 1 strand of embroidery floss and sharp needle.

Yarn Suppliers

Alchemy Yarns
PO Box 1080
Sebastopol, CA 95473
(707) 823-3276
www.alchemyyarns.com
    Fingerless Gloves,
        page 97

Berroco Inc.
14 Elmdale Rd.
Uxbridge, MA 01569-0367
(508) 278-2527
www.berroco.com
    Casual and Dressy Evening
        Bags, pages 75 and 78

Brown Sheep Co. Inc.
10062 Cty. Rd. 16
Mitchell, NE 69357
(308) 635-2198
www.brownsheep.com
    Stimulating Stripes Baby
        Blanket, page 70
    Light and Shadow Blanket,
        page 107

Cascade Yarns
1224 Andover Park East
Tukwila, WA 98188
www.cascadeyarns.com
    Striped Strip Pillow,
        page 42
    Lacy Shrug, page 120

Classic Elite Yarns
122 Western Ave.
Lowell, MA 01851-1434
(978) 453-2837
www.classiceliteyarns.com
    Beaded D Ring Belt,
        page 47
    Ribbed Tie Belt,
        page 49
    Flash Caps, page 93

**Coats & Clark/Aunt
    Lydia's**
PO Box 12229
Greenville, SC 29612-0229
(800) 648-1479
www.coatsandclark.com
    Fancy Foot Thongs,
        page 115
    Trim a Tank Top,
        page 123

Dale of Norway Inc.
N16 W23390 Stoneridge Dr.
Ste. A
Waukesha, WI 53188
(262) 544-1996
www.dale.no
    Vibrant V-Stitch Wrap,
        page 68

Jaeger, see Westminster Fibers
    Handy Utility Cases, page 51

JCA/Reynolds
35 Scales Ln.
Townsend, MA 0
1469-1094
www.jcacrafts.com
    New Direction Scarf,
        page 40

Knitting Fever/Noro
315 Bayview Ave.
Amityville, NY 11701
(516) 546-3600
www.knittingfever.com
    Glamour Girl Cosmetic Bag,
        page 56

Louet Sales (Euroflax)
PO Box 267
808 Commerce Park Dr.
Ogdensburg, NY 13669
In Canada: RR 4, Prescott, ON
    K0E 1T0
www.louet.com
    Farmer's Market Bag,
        page 100

**Muench Yarns Inc./
    Naturwolle/GGH**
1323 Scott St.
Petaluma, CA 94954-1135
(800) 733-9276
www.muenchyarns.com
    Urban Shopper Tote, page 104
    Bobble Clutch Purse, page 117

Plymouth Yarn Co.
PO Box 28
Bristol, PA 19007
(215) 788-0459
www.plymouthyarn.com
    Cashmere Headband, page 62

Rowan Yarns, see Westminster Fibers
    Elegant Chevron Wrap,
        page 64
    Button-Front Top, page 85
    Messenger Bag, page 110

Tahki /Stacy Charles Inc.
70-30 80th St., Bldg. 36
Ridgewood, NY 11385
(800) 338-YARN
www.tahkistacycharles.com
    Quintessential Scarf, page 38
    Neck Gaiter Scarf, page 59
    Funky Stuffed Toys, page 80

**Westminster Fibers Inc./
    Jaeger/Rowan**
4 Townsend West, Unit 8
Nashua, NH 03063
(603) 886-5041
www.knitrowan.com

Index